Surviving Residency

D1565064

Surviving Residency

A medical spouse guide to
embracing the training years

KRISTEN M. MATH

C and B Press

Live it, Write it, Share it

Surviving Residency
A medical spouse guide to embracing the training years

C&B Press books may be ordered through booksellers or by contacting:

C&B Press
1603 Pebble Creek Dr.
Sartell, MN 56377
www.candbpress.com

Because of the dynamic nature of the Internet, any web addresses or links contained in this book may have changed since publication and may no longer be valid. The views expressed in this work are solely those of the author and do not necessarily reflect the views of the publisher, and the publisher hereby disclaims any responsibility for them.

Any people depicted in stock imagery provided by Thinkstock are models, and such images are being used for illustrative purposes only.
Certain stock imagery © Thinkstock.

ISBN-10: 0615781489

ISBN-13: 978-0-615-78148-8

Printed in the United States of America

CONTENTS

Part Four
Financial Survival

Part Five
Relocation

Part Six
Surviving Call

This book is written in honor of all the medical spouses who are out there in the trenches doing the best that they can to support their families and survive the training years.

Acknowledgements

The word gratitude has taken on new meaning for me over the last few years. I thought that my journey as a resident's wife would be the greatest challenge of my adult life. Once our family had finally settled into the new *normal* of life after training, things smoothed out and it began to feel like we had finally achieved the equilibrium that we had sought after for so many years. All of this changed overnight when I was diagnosed with cancer during my pregnancy with our youngest child. Getting through that experience is what inspired me to finally sit down and finish Surviving Residency. I am so grateful to the many people in my life who have stood by me and helped my family to endure and then to move forward.

I am especially thankful to all of my friends at the *international Medical Spouse Network*. You have all been there for me through the highest of highs and the lowest of lows in my life. Thank you for encouraging me to never lose hope and to find the positive in the most difficult of times. I consider myself truly blessed to have you as a part of my extended family.

Dr. David Silverman encouraged me as a young graduate student at the University of Florida. He pushed me to help me to achieve my goals. His support, dedication as a mentor, and acknowledgement of my hard work are things that I continue to be grateful for.

Luanne Hill-Goldberg took the time to read through first drafts of this manuscript and offer me her guidance and helpful suggestions. I am grateful for her friendship and support.

Michele Nelligan listened patiently to my concerns about the second edition and offered me much needed direction.

Elizabeth Anderson is an inspiration to me. When I was undergoing chemotherapy, she helped me to get my children to school during the roughest times, and kept my spirits up with her visits and witty sense of humor. She is the keeper of our house key and has full and unfettered access to the chaos. Her final text revisions allowed me to pull the book together. I am lucky to have her in my life.

My dear friend, Kelly Barnett, helped me to survive fellowship and encouraged me to go after my dreams. I am so blessed to have such a good friend to continue to share the highs and lows of marriage and parenting with. Without her, this book would never have taken shape.

I also would like to thank my good friend Heidi Lamoreaux for her cover art inspiration. She is the designer behind the new cover. After working on the cover, she sat down with the most recent edition and went over it again for errors. I greatly appreciate her support.

The doctors and nurses at St. Cloud Hospital will always have a special place in my heart for their compassionate, competent care. I am particularly grateful to Dr. Barbara Bollinger, Dr. Mark Hauge, Dr. Leland Lindquist, Dr. Jodi Regan, Dr. Eric Thompson, Dr. Louis Heck and Dr. Kathleen Kulus for working above and beyond the call of duty to ensure the best possible outcome for my family during treatment and beyond.

I would like to extend a special thank you to Jean Rafferty, who supported me through my chemotherapy treatments and helped me to move forward with my life after cancer.

I owe a debt of gratitude to Charlene Forsyth for teaching me to let go. The second edition would not have evolved without her support.

I would also like to thank my dad and stepmom, Bob and Rose Baird for going over rough drafts of this manuscript with a fine tooth comb, and for helping me to polish the final project. I feel very fortunate to have them in my life to share fried turkey or debate politics.

I owe my mom, Lois Wilderman, a special debt of gratitude for her daily encouragement during this project and her proofreading and suggestions. She is always there for me when I need her. Thank you, Mom.

My children Andrew, Amanda, Alex, Aidan and Zoe are my inspiration. The joy that they bring to my life each day fills me up with a purpose and motivates me to be the best person that I can.

I am most grateful to my husband, Thomas, who has been my greatest cheerleader. He believed in my ability to finish writing even when I had lost faith in myself. My life began the day that I met you, Thomas.

Preface

I met my husband, Thomas, when I was living abroad in Germany as a foreign exchange student. He was in the middle of his medical school clerkships and I was engaged in a two-semester college internship on one of the hospital's units. It wasn't love at first sight. The truth is that we couldn't stand each other when we first met. I thought he was an arrogant German. He assumed that because I was from America, I chewed gum and drank Coca-Cola. During those early weeks of working together, we exchanged more criticisms than compliments. Despite the fact that we didn't seem to get along, we walked to the cafeteria together each day and sought each other out to discuss patients and other work-related issues. As we spent more time together, a friendship slowly blossomed between us.

Eventually, Thomas asked me out on a first date. We met at his apartment for breakfast. He prepared a traditional German meal of breads, cheeses and marmalade. I brought Fruity Pebbles and milk. After breakfast, we went for a long walk in the woods near his home. As we held hands and talked about our lives, we both knew that we wanted to spend our lives together. We planned our future, shared our dreams, and decided to get married on our first date.

The minister at our wedding put it best: "Berg und Tal kommen nicht zusammen, aber die Leute". *Mountains and Valleys don't come together, but people do.* He elaborated on how people who are very different can complement and enrich each other. This has held true throughout the course of our marriage.

One year later, Thomas had begun residency as an intern. We were married and expecting our first child. In the years that have followed, we have made two international moves and have relocated multiple times within the United States for residency and fellowship. We have been blessed by the births of our five children who range in age from four to sixteen years. Our busy household also boasts three cats, a dog, an African clawed frog and a soft shell turtle, Fred.

Surviving residency and fellowship was one of the biggest challenges that I have faced as an adult. As a newlywed, I craved the companionship of my best friend. I missed him during the hard months when it seemed like he was always at the hospital. I was overwhelmed by the responsibility of taking care of the children and the house on my own. There were times when I thought that I couldn't do it anymore. I was disappointed to discover that there were few resources available for spouses struggling to keep the family running smoothly during the stress of medical training.

After my husband finished his fellowship and accepted a post-training job, I began the process of putting together a reference to help other spouses in the trenches of medical school and residency training. *Surviving Residency* is a labor of love. It contains suggestions and resources that I have collected and used in my journey as a medical spouse. My own life and marriage are far from perfect, and I don't always practice what I preach, but it is my sincere hope that this guide will be a valuable resource for you as you navigate your own way through the training years.

Kris

Foreword to the Second Edition

It has been three years since the initial publication of *Surviving Residency*. In that time, I have gratefully accepted suggestions from readers who took the time to point me towards some of the editing errors that made it through the last round of revisions. I have tried to incorporate as many changes as I could to the content of the book as well. Thank you for all of your ideas.

In the second edition of *Surviving Residency*, many of the errors that escaped us in the editing process the first time around have been fixed (and I'm sure a few new ones have been added). Unfortunately, I was forced to remove the appendix detailing telecommuting jobs. As you know, websites come . . . and websites go. Most of the telecommuting job websites . . . went. In an effort to keep the book as valid and up-to-date as possible, it was necessary to retire that information. Other web links were updated and changed to reflect the most recent and accurate web addresses available. The medical spouse alliance information was corrected and when possible, mailing addresses were added to supplement any website information that might become outdated.

I am very thankful to all of you who took the time to send me messages about errors, information about your medical spouse alliance, or who made suggestions on improving the content. I will continue to work to keep the book updated, so please feel free to contact me through my website **www.kristenmath.com** if there are changes that you would like to suggest for the third edition.

Introduction

We often joke that there are two seasons here in Minnesota: Winter . . . and . . . Construction. It would be funny if it weren't for the fact that we spend roughly six months out of the year confined to our homes and the other six months in reckless pursuit of as much time on our lakes, in our gardens, and walking through our neighborhoods as possible. For almost half of the year we suffer through the isolation and brave the cold with one thought in our minds . . . summer. Of course, when summer comes, we are so busy reconstructing our lives and rebuilding our roads that by the time we finally slow down to catch our breath, winter is already upon us yet again.

It seems like the only people that really get things right here are the diehard fisherman who cast their lines from the shore when the weather is warm and then drive their SUV's out onto the frozen lakes in the dead of winter. Sure, we laugh at them while they set up their tents on the ice to drill holes and bait their hooks, but ultimately, these old school Minnesotans can teach us all a thing about striking a balance in our lives.

Residency has two seasons: Winter and Construction

There are really bad months, where it seems like your spouse is living at the hospital. Medical students and residents work long, unforgiving hours. Pagers interrupt family time, date nights, and much needed sleep. When things are at their worst, it feels like one day bleeds into the next. The effect of this cycle of sleep deprivation and chronic stress can feel like a crushing blow to your relationship and family life.

When you feel like you have been stretched to your breaking point, a new rotation begins. Your spouse might enter a more forgiving clinical month where they are home by dinner time. They may begin a laboratory rotation where their schedule is predictable and the pager collects dust on top of the bookshelf. There is time to reconnect and appreciate the life that you are building before the next month, when the demands change again.

In reality, highs and lows are a part of the natural ebb and flow of marriage, family and life in general. The medical training years present unique challenges that test even the strongest relationships. Medical school and residency training require a commitment of time and emotional resources that can leave little room for family. Physicians in training are required to take call. This means that they have to work over night at the hospital on a regular basis admitting and treating patients. There are exams to study for, procedures to learn, and research that has to be completed. Even with the 80 hour work week rules firmly in place, many students and residents find that they are exhausted by the relentless cycle of stress.

Coping with the extreme highs and lows inherent to residency training presents the ultimate challenge. How do we create balanced, happy lives when we are catapulting from Q4 (every fourth night) call to Q3 (every third night) call? How can we keep our relationships healthy, and our children well-adjusted when we are riding a roller coaster that seems to have no end?

The goal, ultimately, is to be like the old fisherman . . . In the midst of the chaos of medical training, we must find equilibrium, so that instead of living through a process of tearing down and rebuilding, we are able to find a sense of balance in our day-to-day lives. This requires a certain level of acceptance and planning, but ultimately it is possible to take control of our lives and find peace with training.

Part One
The Medical Marriage

Getting married is easy.
Staying married is more difficult. Staying happily married for a
lifetime should rank among the fine arts.
—Roberta Flack

There's a Muppet song called *Somebody's Getting Married.* In *The Muppets Take Manhattan*, as Kermit the Frog and Miss Piggy were united as frog and pig, the celebration of the future ahead of them was commemorated with a fanfare of music and flowers that only Hollywood can deliver. We were assured that their union would effortlessly create happiness, comfort and love for the rest of the days of their lives. Their joy was contagious. If only marriage and relationships were truly this easy to maintain.

In the midst of it all, the Muppet babies sang "Days go passing into years" and the older Muppet ladies reflected that "Years go passing day by day".

Years. Go passing day by day.

It doesn't feel like years are passing day by day when you are in the middle of a month of Q3 call and your children have the flu. There are monthly rotations where it feels like minutes are passing by month by month. It is easy to lose sight of the present and focus on the future when we are struggling to just get through today.

I can't tell you how many times I heard "it will all be worth it someday" from well-intentioned family members or friends when I complained about a holiday missed, or another birthday celebrated alone. It was my thirtieth birthday, in case you want to commiserate. The obvious implication of others was that at the end of training we would hit a special doctor jackpot that would make up for the many milestones in our marriage that we had missed and the mountain of debt that we seemed to effortlessly acquire. Yet, as much as it irritated me to hear that from others, I admit that I clung to the idea that if we could just make it through the USMLe's, internship year, residency, fellowship, (insert your own if here) that things would be better. We would iron out any wrinkles in our relationship later.

We lived for tomorrow.

The focus of our lives narrowed itself to the next rotation, the end of one year of training or the beginning of the next one, and other residency milestones. As a result, our relationship with each other began to look more like an episode of *Roseanne* than *Leave it to Beaver* (not that I ever resembled June Cleaver in the first place though). We had given ourselves permission to stop living in the moment. Instead of working on keeping our marriage strong, we were just struggling to survive the next medical training hurdle. In retrospect, I realize that our life together was being shaped by the training process and how we handled it. We spent too much time living for the future instead of realizing that our life together was happening right then and there and that we were missing it.

Keeping a relationship strong is a challenge for any couple. Statistics tell us that as one couple is getting married, another is threading those marriage vows into a giant matrimony shredder. Medical training presents additional stressors that add to the work of maintaining a healthy balance in a relationship. Taking control of your lives during medical training will give you the best chance to emerge on the other side feeling stronger as a couple. The best way to handle these issues is to be prepared and to face them with honesty and an open mind.

Chapter 1

Connecting in a vacuum

A successful marriage is an edifice that must be rebuilt every day. —
Andre Maurois

There is nothing about the nature of spending years taking Q3 call that establishes the foundation for a strong marriage. Educating a well-trained internist? Definitely. Refining the skills of a sought after surgeon? Absolutely. Requiring a resident to work every third night, all night long, for months or years, places demands on their time that makes a balance between family life and work nearly unattainable. At the same time, becoming a well-qualified physician requires this level of dedication to the training process. Consequently, the resident may be exhausted and on the verge of burnout and as spouses we can become overwhelmed by trying to keep the household running and the family intact.

It reminds me of the Greek legend of Sisyphus. As a punishment for tricking the Gods, Sisyphus was sentenced to a life of pushing a boulder to the top of a mountain. When he reached the peak, the boulder rolled back to the bottom and he had to begin his task all over again. Residency can feel like a never-ending exercise of adjusting to call schedules and pushing on to the next month. Too often, it becomes more about surviving the next rotation and less about patients, medicine, or family. For those of you whose spouses are in a surgery residency and are still pulling those months of illegal Q2 call, I can only tip my hat in respect.

Even more disturbing than the malignant nature of the demands placed on a resident and their family that are inherent to medical training is the failure of the medical establishment to acknowledge and address the effect that the resident's chronic sleep deprivation and absence from home has on the relationship, marriage, or family. It may or may not be possible to transform medical education into a more family-friendly process. Medicine is not, and will never be, a 9-5 job. Patients give birth in the middle of the night, and emergencies can bring doctors back into the hospital during a trip to the movie theater or the family dinner hour. At the same time, acknowledging the challenges faced by those immersed in medical training would open up an honest discussion about finding better ways to strike a balance between the professional demands of a career in medicine and the physician's personal needs and family obligations. Instead, it seems that unnecessary blame is even occasionally placed upon the spouses by malignant residency programs who view the spouse's needs as a detriment to the resident, instead of recognizing how beneficial a supportive relationship can be. Fortunately, this is the exception rather than the rule.

Lack of time together is at the root of many of the problems experienced in the medical marriage. There is less time for communication, intimacy, family or simply relaxing. As a result, couples often enter a survival mode.

Organization replaces intimacy.
Instead of living life, you have to pencil it in.

To survive as a couple it is necessary to find ways to connect emotionally each day despite call schedules, rounds or studying for upcoming boards. There are many simple ways to make the most of the time that you do have together. It cannot be repeated enough times that this might not be the way that you imagined these years in your marriage to be, but that it is important to make the best of the situation that you have in order to grow as a couple. Years from now, you will look back on these days with nostalgia about the way things were.

Have breakfast together

I'm not a morning person, so this advice is slightly hypocritical. This is one of the many examples of *do as I say, not as I do*, that will be nestled in the pages of this book. My inability to get moving in the morning is well-known by friends, teachers and even our cat, Lupie, who sleeps on my pillow and I'm sure sometimes hits the snooze button himself. Even if you aren't a morning person, getting up early with your spouse can be a good way to connect at the beginning of the day. With time at a premium, any opportunities that you might have to communicate about what is going on in your lives are worth trying out. Catch up on the residency program gossip, argue about politics, share an intimate moment, or just enjoy each other's company.

Your morning will likely set the tone for the rest of your day so it makes sense that it is a good idea to avoid arguments about money, call schedules or any disappointments that you may be feeling. Obviously, there is a place for those discussions and you will want to give them the time and attention that they deserve when you are able to work on resolving them.

Connect throughout the day

They say that absence makes the heart grow fonder. I believe this only applies when the object of our affection doesn't burst through the door, drop their dirty scrubs on our freshly folded laundry and then proceed to sleep like the living dead on the sofa for the next twelve hours before going back to work. During a rough call month, there may be days that you will not even see your spouse. With your spouse working all night at the hospital, connecting at all during those times seems out of the question. Touching base with each other throughout the day will help you both to maintain an emotional connection to each other.

Schedule a time when you can call each other to check in each day. The *when* will of course depend a lot on the rotation that they are on, but it is important to maintain daily communication. Even a quick *hello, I'm off to the Operating Room* or *the kids and I are going swimming* will keep you in each other's thoughts. It is important to maintain that level of intimacy. Sharing about your day will help you to stay sympathetic to what you are each experiencing. My husband only has to listen to the kids arguing in the background to know that it's been a long day. If he calls in the late afternoon and hasn't even had time to get lunch yet, I can appreciate that he needs some TLC too.

Back in the days when the dinosaurs roamed the earth and my husband was doing residency, cell phones were a rare commodity. We didn't own them. I had to come up with a unique way to page him to give him a message. We had a simple system. If I paged him 911 it meant *Emergency: call me back right now*. Typing in 111 meant *I love you*. With the advent of text messaging, communicating important information without interrupting clinic or patient visits has become a lot easier.

Another creative way to stay connected is to write each other letters. These can be read at any time during the day and give you time to think about your feelings instead of reacting to situations that arise. Write a little note to say *I love you*, or to share your feelings about an issue in your lives. Some of our worst fights during residency were solved with the pen instead of the sword. Writing out the problem was cathartic for me. After taking the time to put my thoughts on paper, I usually realized what the real source of my frustration was. Often, I was able to calm down and refocus my effort and more calmly address my concerns.

Go to the hospital for dinner on call nights

Hospital food aside, this is a great idea. Frequently, when my husband had call, the children and I joined him for dinner in the cafeteria. At times, I prepared an easy meal and brought it to the hospital with me, but more often than not we ate the standard cafeteria food. This was a little less desirable in the UK, where it seemed every meal was fried in the same oil, but we even enjoyed a Christmas meal in Pennsylvania once that put my own cooking to shame. Recently, my husband had a tough month. He was going in early and coming home after bedtime. My daughter, who spent half of her childhood in his call room, said "If this keeps up we're going to have to go to the hospital and have dinner with him." I realized as we talked how much visiting her dad when she was younger had had a positive impact on her and how important it is to my children that they have their dad as a regular part of their lives.

Planning a trip to the hospital cafeteria at the right time can be tricky. There were times that I got the kids dressed and into the car, drove to the hospital and met him in the cafeteria only to have his pager go off as I unbuttoned the baby's coat. Sometimes we were able to wait in his call room until he was finished seeing the patient and at other times we simply headed back home. Either way, the attempts were worth it. We actually celebrated several birthdays and holidays in the hospital cafeteria and his call room. If you are worried that *people just don't do that* where you are, let me add that you can be the one to change that. Be a trendsetter. You don't need to feel guilty about coming in to eat with your spouse unless you are interfering with their ability to get the job done.

Embrace the situation that you have. You can't change the call schedule, but you can make the best of it.

Institute a regular date night

It is important to spend quality time together as a couple. Healthy relationships grow as we share our life experiences together. The training years can rob us of important opportunities to connect emotionally if we aren't proactive in carving out time together. If you are each working separate jobs, or you are home raising the children during training, then it's important to actively work to spend time together and prevent the relationship from growing apart.

This might seem like a no-brainer to you, or maybe it feels awkward. Planning a date night to reconnect sounded like an exhausting idea to me during residency. I didn't want to have to plan an evening out to spend time together. I wanted our couple time to be natural and easy. I realized though that I was missing our evening walks to get an ice cream cone, time bathing the babies and bedtime routines. We rarely watched our favorite shows together anymore or enjoy the natural ebb and flow of daily life. Sometimes, I worried that we were growing apart. For me, the date night ultimately did become a time to reconnect with each other and share some of what I felt was missing in our lives.

If you have small children, you are probably aware of how difficult it can be to preserve any precious couple time. Children are a wonderful blessing, but their needs can add a wrinkle to any date night plan. Finding a babysitter can be a significant obstacle, but paying for one during residency can be like jumping over a hurdle with two broken legs. If you don't have the money, you just can't do it. Get out your crutches because taking some time to focus on each other and having some alone time together is an essential part of staying connected as a couple. Find a friend with children and do some child-swapping, form a babysitting co-op, or set aside a small amount from each paycheck to be able to afford a babysitter once a month. Last year, our new washing machine began making terrible noises. A quick visit from our appliance repair service revealed that our motor was stuffed full of coins. Our machine had collected $38.75 in change over the course of a year. It was a lose-lose moment, because we paid more than $100 for the repair, but it also served as a reminder that the little change can add up. You can nickel and dime yourself into a date night by carefully checking pockets and filling up a piggy bank in the laundry room.

Here is another honest moment. We rarely had extra money to pay for babysitters during residency. We did occasionally child swap with another couple, but getting schedules to match could be a real challenge. As a result, our date nights took a different form than might be traditionally expected. Because our children were small, we bundled them up at bedtime and took them for a long walk in their buggy, or for a ride in the car. Once they had drifted off to sleep, it was possible for us to spend some alone time walking and talking or at the drive-in movie enjoying a rare movie moment. It wasn't perfect, but it worked.

It isn't important what you do, just that you are doing it together as a couple. Whatever you do, don't neglect your date night.

Establish a niche for yourself

This advice seems out-of-place, and yet focusing on your own life really can make your relationship stronger. In the early years of my husband's training, I spent a lot of time waiting for him to come home. I was often disappointed because he was exhausted and wanted some time for himself. I had been busy with the kids all day and was eager for adult conversation. Secretly, I also wanted him to help me get the dinner ready and the children into bed. I needed him to come through the door and be there for me and more often than not, he simply did not have the energy. This was particularly true if he was post-call.

As I met more people and became more involved in the community, I found that I spent less time waiting for him. Slowly, as my life evolved and I began taking classes at the nearby college and was more engaged in our local medical spouse alliance, I felt more fulfilled. It was easier for me to give him that time at the end of the day to regroup and to tolerate his absence. I felt less resentful of the time that he spent away and as an added bonus, I had many interesting stories to tell him about when we did have time to ourselves. The more important benefit is that I felt happier personally and was better able to cope with the stress of training. If you aren't taking care of yourself and your own needs, you may end up feeling resentful and angry. This will make it harder to connect with your spouse in a positive way.

Finding a niche for yourself might be as easy as getting involved in your local church. Another option is to join the local medical spouse alliance group to get to know other spouses who are going through similar experiences. Many medical spouse organizations have regular meetings, established playgroups, dinner clubs and more. Check with your spouse's medical school or residency program's Office of Medical Education. There are often well-established groups that welcome new members. In addition, the American Medical Association has a national spouse's alliance that is active in most states. To find an alliance organization in your state, visit the AMA Alliance website.

> **AMA Alliance**
> **www.amaalliance.org**
> The AMA Alliance website provides information about local Alliance networks and offers an email newsletter and Listserv.

If there is no medical spouse support group at your program, start one. Chances are that there are many spouses who would be interested in getting involved. You can get an informal group off the ground. Select a date and time for an initial meeting to meet potential members and then work with the Office of Medical Education to get information to prospective spouses. At your first meeting you can decide on a regular time to meet, goals for the organization, and select officers for the year. If you are interested in starting a formal group associated with the American Medical

Association Alliance, contact their organization for information and help.

Recognize that this is temporary ... but don't wish it away

It is easy to lose perspective when you are in the middle of a stressful rotation or are just having a hard time. Nothing screams therapy quite like spending countless hours by yourself in a new town, while you are trying to adjust to changing monthly call schedules. When you have had a chance to recover from a hard month, things will get easier.

These years really are passing by day by day. Before you know it, residency and fellowship will be a distant memory. It's important to define your goals for yourself and your relationship and to work to create happiness in your lives despite the roller coaster of medical training.

Be careful about wishing this time away, because you can never get these years back. Cherish the moments of bringing babies home from the hospital, celebrating birthdays and anniversaries and all of the firsts that go along with a new marriage or young children. Letting the stresses of residency rob you of these moments in time would be the greatest loss of all.

Chapter 2

Navigating marriage
from the trenches

The most important thing in communication
is to hear what isn't being said.
—Peter F. Drucker

Communication is the biggest weak point my husband and I have as a couple. He spends his day at the hospital rounding on patients and comes home drained and in need of some time to unwind. Instead, our clan of kids greets him with smiles, shrieks and teen grumbles. I, on the other hand, spend my day shuttling around children. I listen to their problems, clean up their messes, change their diapers and help with homework. I wouldn't change it for a second, but at the end of the day (and sometimes by lunch time), I'm just too exhausted to engage in a discussion about any issues going on in our lives . . . big or small.

With five children and busy lives, there is always something that needs to be discussed. If it isn't the transmission quitting on me when I'm driving the kids to school (in my pajamas of course), then it is the bills for the orthodontist, an unpleasant surprise at school conferences or the hail storm that shot golf ball-sized hail pummeling onto our roof. All of these issues require us to pull together as a team and work through the details. In times of stress though, when my husband is working until the evening hours, playing the role of grown-up can be hard.

Talk

Make some time each day to touch base about the ongoing issues in your life. Talk about the big stuff. Talk about the little stuff. Share about school schedules, children's activities, or your hopes and dreams for the future. Make it a point to have a discussion as often as possible about things that are important to you both. Even short conversations between pages on a call night can help to keep the lines of communication open.

Try to steer clear of the major communication pitfalls that can occur in all relationships that are subjected to prolonged stress:

✓ Avoid swearing: Respect yourself enough to keep the potty words at bay.

✓ Keep your voice down: No one listens when we're yelling anyway.

✓ Don't pull out the big guns: Throwing out the word divorce, even if you feel like you mean it at the time because you are so stressed out, opens the door to a new low. Once the word has escaped, it can never really be taken back.

The key to healthy communication is respect. It's important to talk to each other the way that we want to be talked to, without blaming, demeaning or putting each other down. That seems pretty straight-forward, but sometimes putting these obvious concepts into practice can be difficult. Effective communication takes effort and practice. The more you talk with each other to solve problems or ideas, the better you will become at it. The pitfall here is that the more that you practice dysfunctional ways of talking with each other, the more deeply engrained these habits can also become.

This is not something that I always do well. One of the worst fights my husband and I had happened during the early years of his internal medicine residency. We had a rare evening to ourselves without children and were walking through the city center after all of the shops had closed. Instead of making a conscious effort to enjoy our time, we started arguing about everything that felt wrong in our lives. In German. Loudly. I would guess that we spent an hour looping around the shops yelling at each other. At some point, we noticed that an older couple was keeping pace with us. In our frustration and anger, we continued arguing. Finally, my husband turned to me, told me how much he loved me, and wrapped his arms around me. Within two minutes, the couple that had been following us rushed over and began speaking to us . . . in German. They had been married many years and had survived similar arguments. My embarrassment quickly turned to shame as I realized how ugly my words must have sounded. This was one of my many *aha* experiences. I vowed to do better and to try and think about the impact of my words before I said them.

To be honest, it has taken me years to get to a point where I can take a deep breath before overreacting and pushing an argument to the next level. Sometimes I have to give myself a time out where I go for a walk and then return to a discussion once I've cleared my head and have gotten a little bit of exercise. Whatever works to keep emotions from spiraling out of control (as long as it isn't harmful) is worth doing.

Be prepared to listen

This is the most difficult aspect of communicating from my perspective. I will be the first to admit that I am more likely to spend days coming up with a litany of complaints and frustrations that I feel need to be addressed. If left unchecked, I am likely to *communicate* my frustrations without really taking the time to hear my husband's perspectives, needs, or feelings.

The ability to actively listen to your spouse when they share their experiences and feelings about training is one of the most important lessons in communication. Talking is easy. Hearing what someone else is trying to say can be very challenging, especially when you are both experiencing stress. Here are some basic communication tips:

- ✓ Ask your spouse questions about their thoughts and feelings about training and be prepared to really hear their responses.

- ✓ Turn off the computer or the television and give your spouse your full attention so that they understand that you are willing to focus on their needs. If you're listening to your favorite radio show while you cook dinner, you will be too distracted to pay attention.

- ✓ Make eye contact with your spouse and then use your body language to show that you are listening. Touch their arm or gesture with a hand. Make an effort to respond to your spouse in a way that shows that you are interested in their feelings or thoughts. It's ok to interject with a "really" or "no way" so that they know you are listening.

- ✓ Pay attention to body language. Can you tell just by looking at your spouse that they are sad or angry or happy? "You seem really angry about that" is one way to signal that you are engaged in the discussion.

I reached a point during residency where I blamed my husband for how I was feeling. I couldn't recognize anymore that he was experiencing similar stresses and exhaustion. It hit me like a lightning bolt one evening during a particularly angry exchange we were having. While I was spouting out my laundry list of complaints, he interjected, "How do you think I feel?" I was actually startled by this question. It hadn't occurred to me that he might be struggling with the same issues that I was. I began to realize that instead of seeing my husband as my ally, I had begun to regard him with the same contempt that I viewed the hospital that was holding him hostage. When I really started listening to how he was feeling and to the experiences that he was having on the units, I became less resentful and aggressive in my approach. I began again to feel that he was my friend and partner again.

Recognize that you are in this experience together and that you each have certain basic needs that must be met. Ask your spouse what they need from you in order to help them to manage the stress of training. Become a partner in their residency by asking them about their rotation, their colleagues and their feelings. Besides connecting you to your spouse's residency on a new level, it may just make for some interesting dinner conversations.

Pick your battles and be realistic

That old cliché about picking your battles really is true. At some point I realized that no matter how much I nagged, there were certain expectations that I had of my spouse that just weren't going to be met. Instead of listening to my expectations, my husband even began to shut me out. For us, the most recent issue revolved around household chores. I wanted him to step up to the plate and help out more, and he did. The only problem that I had with this is that he chose the jobs that were interesting to him and left the less desirable ones for me. To top it off, he had begun folding laundry. I am very particular about not only *how* I fold, but the order that I place folded laundry into the baskets to put away. His method is to roll clothing into balls and then stuff them into drawers. I wasted many hours refolding and chastising him for his complacency. Why couldn't he take the time to do things right (my way, of course)? Soon, I noticed that the mountains of laundry were being left for me to fold alone again. It didn't take me long to appreciate his help and to recognize that I needed to change my expectations and be grateful for the help that I was getting. There are so many issues in our lives where it is important for me to take a stand, and laundry just isn't one of them.

It is easy to get caught up in your expectations and ideas of how you want things to be without considering the reality of the situation at hand. Yes, he promised to take the garbage out and forgot again, but is it worth the argument? It would be nice if she could help clean the house on her day off, but would giving her a few extra hours to sleep mean spending quality time together later? Ultimately, it's important to analyze your objectives.

I'm not suggesting giving your spouse a free pass by any means, but the reality of the situation is that you may have to lower your expectations during tough call months in order to keep the peace. As tempting as it sometimes is to demand that your spouse do their fair share of the work around the house, it is necessary to understand that the fair share for a medical student or a resident might be different from the fair share for someone in a less demanding profession.

I'll be the first to admit that I felt that there was a great deal of injustice in this. Earlier in our marriage I remember responding with anger. I felt that he had chosen this path for us and that while our entire lives revolved around him and his career, I was the one having to do the work to keep things going. While he was studying for the boards, I was the one taking care of the children, calling the plumber, mowing the lawn and taking the car in to be repaired. It felt like the responsibility for managing every aspect of our lives together fell squarely on my shoulders. When it came time to move, I managed all of the details, packed the entire house and did all of the painting and cleaning. It felt overwhelming to me and I was angry.

My feelings were justified, but dragging them around with me and wallowing in them served no valuable purpose. The truth is that we both had chosen this. My husband was working hard to establish a career and support his family. He felt just as exhausted and abused by the system as I did. As I began to realize this, I was able to let go of some of my bitterness.

It is important to understand that you are both in this together for the long haul. It might not be easy and it won't always be fair. That is a hard pill to swallow. We are sold certain ideas about what the modern marriage should be like, and for all practical purposes, the training years do not reflect that image.

Cut yourself some slack too. You are working hard and if the kitchen floor isn't clean enough to eat off of or the beds don't get made, it isn't the end of the world. Be realistic about what you can accomplish without feeling resentful and find a way to let the rest go.

If someone had taken a snapshot of my marriage at any given time during training it would have presented a distorted picture. I seemed to be making most of the sacrifices. If you were to zoom out and take a picture of my whole marriage though, you would see that things have evened themselves out. With the rigors of medical school, residency and fellowship behind us, my husband now has much more time and emotional energy to devote to our marriage and our family.

The frustrations, loneliness and exhaustion of medical training are just a snapshot in time. These feelings are valid, but they don't have to define your whole relationship.

Bury the hatchet

We were getting ready to move for fellowship and my grandmother became critically ill. I pulled out the quilt that she had made for me when I was a little girl and sat down in the basement next to the half-packed boxes and cried. I cried because I knew that she was dying. I cried because residency was over and we were moving again for fellowship into the unknown. I comforted myself that night alone in the basement with the love that had been placed in careful stitches in each block of the quilt.

Later that week, I went down to do more packing and the quilt was gone. I looked everywhere for it while my husband sat silently upstairs in the living room. When he finally came downstairs to help me pack, the gentle touch of his hand on my back told me everything that I needed to know. He hadn't realized how important it was to me and had thought that I had taken it out of the box to put it in the *throw away* pile.

I was devastated by what I perceived to be his thoughtlessness and betrayal, and it honestly took me years to stop bringing that up every time that we had a fight. If I'm honest, there are still times that I can't resist. The truth of the matter is that no amount of crying or anger will bring the quilt back. It was an unintentional mistake and after nine years it does nothing to the argument at hand but elevate it into a mudslinging competition.

Letting go of past hurts can be hard, but it is necessary to forgive your spouse or yourself and move forward. Bringing up the past can only hurt the present.

Make a decision to find forgiveness. Maybe your spouse has said or done something that is unkind, or you have lashed out in a moment of vulnerability. What are you going to do about it? You can choose to harbor a grudge or feel angry or guilty, or you can try to understand the behaviors, find empathy and move forward. Ask for forgiveness and offer up forgiveness of your own. Start over; recognizing that once you have forgiven each other, it isn't fair to rehash the old issues. If the problems seem too overwhelming or it is not possible to come to a peaceful resolution on your own, seek out the help of a counselor. Do what you have to do to keep your relationship strong.

Managing conflict

If your arguments tend to deteriorate into battles that leave you both licking your wounds and wondering whether or not you can survive, you are not alone. Our most dramatic disagreement involved a home renovation project gone terribly wrong. The work should have been done by Halloween. Instead, Halloween day we still had workers in our home. For me, the day was a complete wash. I spent my day chasing children and pets to keep them away from the saws, running to doctor's appointments and dealing with renovation issues. Late in the afternoon, we discovered unexpectedly that we would have to book a hotel room because of fumes from our newly finished floors. In the midst of this chaos, I was trying to get Halloween costumes on my children and pack overnight bags when I discovered that my 3 year old had lost his all-important skeleton mask.

At just this moment, my husband walked through the door oblivious to what had been going on and proceeded to argue with me about booking a hotel room for the evening. I lost it. The workers saws stopped their horrible screech and though I could hear them walking towards the top of the stairs for a better ringside seat, I couldn't hold back the floodwaters that had risen up and consumed me. I assure you that they all had interesting stories to go back and tell their own spouses.

To say that I was embarrassed is an understatement. I have worked hard to learn how to handle conflict more effectively, but moments like that drive home the uncomfortable truth that I still have growing to do. I placate myself by recognizing that many couples have exchanged anger-driven words that they later regret. I know that I'm not alone in feeling badly about an argument, and that it's ok to move forward and work hard to do better the next time. If you are feeling provoked and are on the offensive, consider the following simple exercise to de-escalate your anger.

SCaD: Slow, Calm, and Deliberate

The basic principle of SCaD or the Slow, Calm and Deliberate method of diffusing an argument is to put the power to de-escalate a disagreement into your hands before it turns into an all-out quarrel:

✓ *Slow Down*: Slow down your actions. When we are irritated or upset it follows that we begin moving more quickly. If you find yourself slamming a cupboard door or wiping the countertop furiously, slow yourself down physically. Put down the sponge if you have to. Close the cupboard as quietly as you can. You won't feel less angry initially, but putting the brakes on your movements will help you to gain control.

✓ *Find Calm*: Take a deep breath and compose yourself. If your voice is loud or angry, rein it in and begin talking in lower, slower tones. It might feel awkward at first, but it will go a long way towards helping you feel more composed.

✓ *Be Deliberate*: Consider each word that you say before you say it. Think about how exactly you want to be perceived and the point you are trying to make. Taking just a few seconds to reflect on the potential effect of your words might prevent you from saying something that you will later regret.

At the end of the day, it's important to recognize that the only person that you can change is you. Sometimes though, leading by example can help to initiate a more positive exchange by both partners.

Our Halloween wasn't a complete disaster. I took the kids trick-or-treating and we made it to the hotel with our costumes on and our overnight bags in tow. Once we had checked in, I realized that I didn't have pants for my oldest daughter or a shirt for one of my sons. The anger was gone. I accepted defeat and instead of racing out to the store to buy a quick replacement, I declared November 1 a mental health day and we all played hooky and enjoyed spending time swimming and relaxing.

Consider Counseling

Many couples are hesitant to talk with someone about the issues going on in their marriage, but finding a good therapist who has experience working with medical families can be helpful.

During fellowship, my husband and I reached a point where we were barely able to even talk with each other without it becoming a fight. His schedule was outrageous and I felt bitter, angry and resentful about the direction that our lives had taken. I withdrew from him because I felt like the entire focus of our marriage had become about him and his career. The children and I had become more like a footnote in his life. From his perspective, I had become unsupportive, cold and negative. I can't say that this was not accurate.

We only attended a handful of counseling sessions together because of his schedule, but it did help us to say to each other what we were unable to express when we were alone. It forced us to reevaluate what we wanted for our lives. Ultimately, for us, that meant stepping off of the treadmill that we were on to embrace a lifestyle that was more family -friendly. We ended up choosing a post-training position in a less urban area that offered us more time together as a family.

You should consider counseling if:

- ✓ Your feelings of isolation or depression are affecting your ability to work or take care of the kids.

- ✓ Your anxiety about your relationship, parenting or financial issues is affecting your ability to eat or sleep.

- ✓ You and your spouse are fighting all of the time and you have begun to think that you won't make it through residency as a couple.

- ✓ You are struggling with suicidal thoughts or fears of harming yourself.

✓ You are using alcohol or drugs as a way to cope with the daily stress of training or other situations in your life.

✓ Your arguments with your spouse become mean, hurtful or even violent.

✓ You feel like you would benefit from talking with someone and you have read through this checklist to validate to yourself that it is ok to make an appointment.

If you are feeling depressed or think that you and your spouse could benefit from the support of a therapist, don't hesitate to reach out for assistance. Many spouses and medical families have been helped by a little extra support during the training years and beyond.

A large number of residency programs offer free counseling to residents and their families as a part of the benefits package. Though these sessions may be limited in number, they still are likely to be useful. Depending on the issues you are dealing with and your comfort with the level of confidentiality that you will receive, it may be important to you to look outside of the hospital system for help.

If you would like to seek counseling outside of the residency program, the American Association for Marriage and Family Therapy (AAMF) provides a therapist locator directory that can be searched by city.

Therapist Locator
www.therapistlocator.net
The AAMF provides this therapist locator. Enter your area code and search for a certified marriage and family therapist within a 5, 10, 15, 25, 50 or 100 mile radius from your home. Many therapists provide additional information about their practice and therapeutic approaches at the website.

If exploring the AAMF registry doesn't bring you closer to your goal of finding a qualified therapist, there are many other ways to find the right counselor to work with you. Contact your insurance company or primary care physician for a referral. You can also make a call to a local university that offers training programs or specialty clinics in psychology. Describe briefly what you need and follow up on those suggestions. Looking through the yellow pages of your phonebook for individuals who accept your insurance and have experience with the problems you are having, is another alternative.

After you have found a potential provider, schedule an appointment to interview the therapist and determine whether or not they are a good fit for you as an individual or a couple. View your initial consultation as an opportunity to ask questions and find out if you feel comfortable with the provider. There is nothing wrong with interviewing a few different therapists until you find someone that you are able to connect with.

Come up with a communication plan

It is one thing to recognize that the medical training years will be stressful. It is obvious that the lack of sleep, pressure to perform at a high level and the time that your spouse spends away from the family will be a source of disruption. Once you have identified situations that are likely to surface, coming up with an effective plan to communicate with each other during these difficult times is essential to getting through training. Don't wait until you are in the middle of a stressful rotation to come up with a plan to deal with stressful situations.

Use the following communication exercise to help you evaluate your communication style and help you to come up with a plan that will work for you.

Communication Exercise

What are current sources of stress for you and your spouse?
> Call schedules, children, financial strain.

_____
_____
_____

What are your communication coping styles?
> Are you a screamer? Does your spouse avoid confrontation?

_____
_____
_____

Can you anticipate any additional sources of stress during the next month?
> Birthdays, anniversaries, holidays . . .

_____
_____
_____

How can you both handle these situations as a team?
> If you were a fly on the wall, what advice would you give yourself bout communicating more effectively?

_____
_____
_____

What can you each do to effectively diffuse a
situation that is heading towards an argument?

> Think of an argument that you have had
> recently. If you could go back and have the
> same discussion, how would you do it
> differently?

_____

_____

_____

What could your spouse have done to diffuse the
argument?

> Would it help if your spouse gave you a 15
> minute break to sort your thoughts out?
> Are you less likely to lose your temper if
> she avoided criticizing?

_____

_____

_____

What does your spouse need from you in order to
cope more effectively with the stress of training?

_____

_____

_____

What do you need from your spouse in order to
cope more effectively with the stress of their
training?

_____

_____

_____

Chapter 3

Restoring intimacy

Love is not measured by how many times you touch each other but by how many times you reach each other.
—Cathy Morancy

I discovered that I was pregnant with our third child late in the summer of 1998. I wrapped a pair of yellow baby slippers in decorative paper for my husband to open. After we high-fived each other and tried to calculate the due date, one question remained. How the heck did that happen? The running joke during residency was that someone must have put something in the water that created babies. It seemed like everyone was pregnant or had just had a baby. The real irony is that any of us managed to get pregnant at all. With Q3 call schedules and the demands of residency we all were simply too tired for sex when and if the opportunity presented itself.

The struggle to connect both emotionally and sexually certainly goes hand-in-hand with the issue of having less time to spend together. It can be more difficult to maintain a high level of intimacy when your partner has to work long, hard hours and is exhausted. They are too tired, and you may be feeling less connected or more distant because of their frequent absences. Recognizing that emotional and sexual intimacy can suffer during tough months and that many couples during medical training experience this can offer some validation.

Don't take it personally

When my husband started his internship year, he often came home exhausted and fell right into bed to sleep after eating a meal. I often laid there wondering what had become of our passionate pre-residency nights. I decided one day to pull out all the stops and reel him back in. I bought myself a slinky outfit and when he left the hospital to come home I lit candles, placed them strategically throughout the living room and dimmed the lights. He arrived home and walked into the room.

"What is wrong with the lights?" he said, looking directly at me.

He managed to carry on a five minute conversation with me before realizing that I had gone to great lengths to prepare a romantic evening. I couldn't help but feel rejected. I later found out that he had lost his first patient that day, and I realized that his own personal stress was also a factor that affected his ability to connect with me.

It is important to recognize that your spouse's lack of desire is not necessarily a reflection on you or your relationship. Struggling to connect intimately can be an unfortunate consequence of physical and emotional exhaustion. Every couple experiences periods of time where intimacy takes a back seat to other issues. Knowing in advance that this happens and that these fluctuations are normal might help to ease the gnawing fear at the back of your mind that this could be a permanent problem. If you are struggling through a low period, consider connecting to your spouse in different ways.

Work on the emotional connection

One unfortunate and very common side-effect of residency training is that many couples struggle to maintain an emotionally intimate relationship. It's hard to relate on a positive emotional level when time is in short supply and stress is abundant. If you feel lonely, disconnected from your spouse, angry, or like you are sacrificing and aren't getting much in return, one of the first places this can show up is in the bedroom.

Towards the end of my husband's ICU rotation, I vividly remember waking up in the morning and wondering not only how on earth I had gotten myself into this mess but also who the heck that snoring man lying next to me was. I felt like an imposter in my own life. After wallowing in my unhappiness, I spent the day brushing off old photo albums and rekindling an emotional connection that I had feared that I had lost. Reminding myself of why I had fallen in love with my husband and of all of the good times that we had enjoyed together helped reawaken my warm feelings for him. I had some honest moments with myself about the direction that I was taking my life in and about how I was contributing to the unhappiness in our lives. Taking some ownership of the situation helped me to come up with a plan for what I could do to stay more emotionally involved.

If you are feeling detached, take charge of the situation. Only you and your spouse know what is missing in your relationship. If part of the problem stems from not having enough time together without the children, make hiring a babysitter a must. If you are unhappy with the direction of your own life, decide on some short-term goals and then put that plan into motion. Eliminate the background stress that you can, and then focus on reconnecting with each other emotionally. Talk about how you met, play your song on the stereo while you sip a cup of tea, share your future dreams and goals with each other and listen to what the other person needs. The emotional connection that has always been there will restore itself.

Find other ways to show your affection

I am a candlelight dinner followed by a slow-dance girl at heart. Romantic gestures like a box of chocolates or a single rose placed delicately on my pillow make me feel special and appreciated. During the early years of our marriage, my husband and I savored the opportunities to surprise each other with thoughtful expressions of our love for each other. He rubbed my feet when I was pregnant and they ached; I massaged his neck after a long night of call when he couldn't fall asleep. There was an intimate connection that felt unbreakable. Life got busy, and we allowed the stress of residency and fellowship to slowly erode the intimate connection that we had built over the years. We didn't realize that something had changed until our relationship felt like it wasn't working anymore.

Intimacy can take many forms. You can snuggle in front of the television or hold hands when you are at the shopping mall. Small gestures can make a big difference in staying connected with each other and maintaining that sensual bond. Make the most of the time that you have together and explore other ways to be close. Take the time to give that back rub or foot massage. Remove the pressure by making the focus more about showing affection for each other than sex.

Plan a romantic getaway

At first glance this suggestion sounds like a real stretch. After all, we are talking about the medical training years. Getting away for a few days though can be the perfect prescription for improved intimacy. You do not have to go to Mexico or Paris to create a romantic, intimate vacation.

Try planning a night or weekend trip to an area hotel. Enjoy the change of scenery, swim in the pool and order room service. When my mother visited us during residency and fellowship, we often spent a night away while she watched the children. It was inexpensive and gave us the opportunity to watch a movie in bed, and spend time together talking. We both felt more refreshed and sexual intimacy was a natural part of being relaxed and finding an emotional connection again.

You don't have to leave your home to create a vacation environment. If money is in short supply or you can't find a babysitter, turn your home into a relaxing retreat. Change the sheets on your bed, set candles out in the room, dim the lights, add some relaxing music, and throw in a bottle of wine and some cubes of cheese. Enjoy your very own private bed and breakfast.

Schedule Sex

That's right . . . pencil sex into your schedule. This suggestion may at first appear to remove any last shred of romance from your relationship, but that isn't necessarily the case. Look at it as more of an opportunity to take advantage of the times when your spouse's schedule is less demanding.

Evaluate your schedules to determine when you are both likely to be well-rested and more relaxed. Spend time preparing a romantic dinner, picking out that special outfit or plan a romantic night out. Keep your expectations realistic. This is not a high pressure situation. Enjoy your time together without feeling compelled to perform.

Just Do It

During residency training, with time at a premium, sometimes it just doesn't seem like the right time for sex materializes. Stop waiting for the candlelight dinner, soft music, and roses and seize the opportunities that are available. If the kids are asleep and your spouse is up taking a shower, by all means jump into the shower with him. You might not be a morning person, but waking up early one morning to take advantage of the moment might put you both in a good mood for the rest of the day.

Chapter 4

The great balancing act

Marriage should be a duet-when one sings, the other claps.
—Joe Murray

Halfway through my husband's intern year, one of the surgery residency spouses disappeared. One night, after struggling through her husband's demanding call schedule while she stayed at home with three little girls, she simply packed a bag and vanished in the middle of the night. She didn't come back home for three days. Many of us were shocked by her choice, but we also had to admit that during particularly rough call months we had all contemplated making that great escape too.

Medical training is a demanding, sometimes all-consuming process that requires the support of the entire family. It is not unusual for spouses to feel that their own personal and professional needs have taken a backseat. Adjusting to a new equilibrium in the relationship can be frustrating. It is only natural to feel resentful or exhausted at times when you feel that there is little reciprocation. Finding a balance in your relationship is necessary.

Acknowledge the inequity

It is there. It is real. Your feelings are valid.

The spouse that once did their fair share is practically invisible. You are now the one who is taking out the trash, painting the bedrooms, mowing the lawn, caring for the children, and possibly even working outside of the home yourself. Your once blossoming career may have been sidetracked. Instead of accepting that partner position in the big law firm, you may have been forced to accept a less prestigious job. Perhaps you made the choice to become a stay-at-home mom or dad in order to support the family. Whatever your choice was, the equilibrium in your relationship is likely changing.

I chose to stay at home with my son when my husband began training. Through the years though, I also found that my choices were often dictated more by what was realistic for our family than by my own desires. It was hard to accept that what I wanted for my life was often low on the priority list during those times. I realized that I felt envious of my husband. He was working hard as a resident and was becoming more successful, respected and self-confident. I had made the choice to put my career on hold and stay at home with my children while they were young, but I began to feel like I was living in his shadow. Even though I was proud of his accomplishments and happy being a stay-at-home parent, I was also feeling very jealous. This was a painful realization for me and was very difficult for me to admit to myself and to him.

Talking this through with my husband was helpful because it made him realize that I needed validation that my contribution and sacrifices were important. This gave him the opportunity to be more sensitive to my needs. When it was possible, he tried to help me carve out a piece of our lives that belonged to me.

When you are feeling that your career choice, personal or professional aspirations aren't valued as being equally important, it is important to be open about this with your spouse. Whether you are a stay-at-home parent or work outside of the home, your contribution to the stability of your marriage and family is essential and should be celebrated.

Define what you need

You are making sacrifices to support your spouse and your family during these difficult years. It is reasonable to expect that your needs will be taken seriously. Take some time to determine what you need to help you maintain an equitable balance in your personal and professional life.

Perhaps it is important to you that your spouse helps more around the house or is more involved in the day-to-day routines with the children. Come up with a realistic list of tasks together that your spouse can help you with so that the relationship functions more like a team with each person having certain responsibilities. It is essential to recognize that your partner's contribution may not be as substantial as you would like. Choose tasks that are important for you to have done, that are reasonable to complete and that your spouse is willing and able to do. Finally, be flexible about when things need to be accomplished if possible. At the same time, it's important to discuss that you may need the same gift of flexibility with your own busy schedule.

Is your own career is taking a backseat because of the demands of residency or fellowship? At the very minimum, your professional contributions need to be validated as being equally important. If you have had to accept a less desirable position or are working to begin your own career, it might feel like every conversation revolves around residency and fellowship. It's ok to pull the emergency brake and refocus so that the discussions involve you both.

The training years can become an exercise in *me* instead of *we*. If you feel that your relationship has become unbalanced, take some time to determine what needs you have that are going unmet.

Devise a plan

Determine what you and your spouse can do to help get things back on track. Be specific about your needs so that when your spouse is willing or able to lend a hand, you will get what you need in order to feel like your life is more balanced. If you need your spouse to watch the kids while you get a cup of coffee once a week and enjoy an hour or two for yourself, ask for it. Residency and fellowship may interfere with their ability to grant this request, so hiring a babysitter once a week may be a better option.

Maybe you want your spouse to become more involved as a parent when he is home. Come up with a list of suggestions step up to the plate and bathe the children when he is home. Perhaps you want an opportunity to discuss your own career goals without them being dismissed as less important or insignificant. Outline detailed steps that you can take individually and as a couple to create more balance in your relationship and for your own life.

No relationship is perfect. Ups and downs are a normal part of any marriage. It might be important to remind yourself of that when things feel out of balance and you wonder if your relationship is in trouble. The added stress of medical training can exacerbate those highs and lows. Struggling in your relationship does not mean that your marriage isn't strong. To the contrary, it is surviving the hard times together that helps bring us even closer together. The stresses of medical training can seem overwhelming at times, but it is important to keep in mind that many couples start their families, move across the country and struggle to stay afloat during these years. It isn't easy and it requires a great deal of sacrifice from both partners. In the end, the journey is worth it.

Part Two
Parenting

Children are not things to be molded,
but are people to be unfolded.
—Jess Lair

Parenting is in many ways like playing a game of kick ball with my four year old.

"No mom, you're on my team."

"Why did you kick the ball, you're not on my team!" (said before the tears start).

"You have to freeze after you kick the ball."

"Don't move, you're still freeze-ed."

Playing with my daughter requires me to be flexible and go with the flow of the game. In parenting, the rules also feel like they are always changing. There are great debates that emerge every few years about the right way to do things:

- Bottle vs breast
- Spanking vs time-outs
- Family bed vs crying it out

It can be downright frustrating trying to navigate the changes. In my early years of being a mom, I often felt overwhelmed by trying to do things the *right* way. I read parenting books and magazines in search of certainty. I felt that my children would turn out ok if I could only figure out how a *good mom* approaches motherhood. What I have ultimately discovered is that there are a lot of right ways to be a good parent. A parenting method that is effective for one family might not be a good tool for another, so as a general rule, I don't give out parenting advice. If I did, my teenagers would probably laugh so loud that you would hear them anyway.

Every thoughtful comment in this section should be prefaced by "I think", "I hope" and "In my humble and oh-so-limited experience". It may seem unusual that a busy mom of five is confessing to not having a clue, but I sometimes feel that with each child we have had I actually know progressively less about parenting. Whenever I think I have it all figured out, something unexpected happens to open my eyes to how much I still have to learn.

If I do get a little overly-confident and actively dole out advice, karma always has a way of bringing it back to me . . . in spades. The karma began when I told a dear old friend and mom of five that I would never have five children. I was pregnant with my second baby and couldn't understand why anyone would want such a large family. She had the last laugh when I called to tell her that I was pregnant with baby number five.

This is not a how-to section. It is really a collection of ideas that have worked for us and may or may not work for you. Please keep the karma vibes at bay.

Chapter 5

Single parenting 101

Other things may change us,
but we start and end with family.
—Anthony Brandt

Long before our first son came screaming into the world, I knew what kind of mom that I was going to be. I had our family life planned out perfectly, from my extensive birthing plan, which included scented candles, a tape of my favorite songs and big, fluffy pillows, to the cloth diapers and homemade organic food that I was going to make. I was convinced that my husband and I would take leisurely family walks together each weekend, share a nightly meal and that we would stand at the door to our children's rooms each night, admiring them as they drifted off into sleep. He would take me in his arms, and we would marvel over the lives that we had created.

The realities of parenting through residency hit me hard, starting with the birth of our first child.

We didn't have time to get the songs or pillows to the hospital after I was admitted unexpectedly. I ended up having a C-section following almost two days of unproductive labor before our son was delivered. During labor with our second child, my husband was checking in on patients. Within minutes of the birth of our third, he was in his office finishing work. He had to be paged on the overhead hospital system when a serious complication reared its ugly head. The nightly meals and family walks were replaced by trips to the hospital cafeteria. I slowly realized that I was the primary caregiver and that my husband's role as a father at that time could best be considered a bonus instead of a regular contribution. It was a reality that we both reluctantly accepted.

It isn't easy adapting to life as the primary caregiver to a child . . . and a resident physician. Parenthood itself is a life-altering adjustment. Managing all aspects of caring for a young child while your spouse is in training can test the stamina and resilience of any parent.

Be realistic

It is unlikely that you can homeschool your children, keep your house neat as a pin, and prepare gourmet organic meals each night. During the early years of my career as a mom, I desperately wanted to be everything to my children. I made an effort to bake homemade bread every other day. Each year, I tried to sew creative Halloween costumes. I established an educational theme each week for my preschoolers and did related crafts with them. Ultimately, I exhausted myself by setting up unrealistic expectations for what I could accomplish without losing my marbles. Parenthood is not synonymous with omnipotence, regardless of what I might tell my children.

Accepting my own limitations required that I come face to face with my own exhaustion and feelings of failure. After struggling to be the perfect mom that I thought I had to be, I was confronted with the reality that I could still be a good mom even if my house looked like a bomb had exploded in it. If we lived out of the laundry basket one week, the world would not end. My husband would interject here that I have now perfected the art of not worrying about the house or the laundry.

If you are feeling overwhelmed by the demands of parenting and residency, you are not alone. Write out your daily *to-do* list to get a better idea of what you are trying to accomplish. Reduce your daily load by cutting out as much as you can from the list. You can't eliminate a pediatrician appointment, but if your day is already busy, you can choose to make fish sticks and macaroni and cheese for dinner instead of Osso Bucco.

Get organized

The year that my oldest son started high school was a year of firsts for our family. Our youngest daughter was starting preschool, our second youngest child was entering Kindergarten, and our middle child was starting junior high. They were all at different schools on opposite sides of town from each other. My own personal chaos meter was on red alert, and on our family vacation during the last week of summer, one of my children destroyed my iPhone (which contained my detailed calendar) by accidentally spilling root beer on it. I tried to recreate my calendar as best I could, but there were a few glitches. I helped my four year old into her new school dress, pumped her up about starting preschool and drove her to school. We walked in to discover that not only was I a day early, but a meeting of area preschool teachers was underway. My own personal embarrassment aside, it was a wake-up call about my organizational skills. If you consider yourself to be organizationally challenged, take heart. It is possible to get it together with a small amount of planning. Once you take the first steps, keeping up with all of the odds and ends that life throws at you will be much easier.

Getting organized is as easy as investing in a wall calendar and a set of colored pens or downloading the latest calendar application for your mobile phone (just be sure to back it up regularly on your computer). Pick a pen color for each member of your family and begin writing in important dates like nights that your spouse has call, doctor's appointments and any other important events you have going on or set alarms for the events that you add to your digital calendar. The farther in advance you can set up your calendar, the easier it will be to get an overview of your monthly, weekly and daily schedules. Keeping it color-coded will make it even less complicated. If you have children in school, buy a small cabinet with hanging file folders and create a folder for each child to hold school pictures, permission slips, immunization records, social security cards, passports and any other important information. A word to the wise: Plastic filing boxes are a great inexpensive option. Don't buy a metal filing cabinet unless you are ok with it rusting and ruining your carpet. I will spare you the gory details.

Make your life more predictable by choosing a day (or two) each week for laundry or other domestic responsibilities. Scrub the floors on Mondays, dust on Tuesdays and throw the laundry in on Wednesdays and Sundays. Do whatever you need to do to get control of the little things in your life and create a manageable, organized routine.

Simplify meals by developing a weekly plan. Mondays are always pasta nights in our house. It isn't glamorous, but at the beginning of the week, I need something easy to make that will fit into our busy schedule. Some Monday nights we have spaghetti and meatballs. If I'm feeling energetic, I might do a vodka penne pasta. Monday is not negotiable. It is always, predictably pasta.

Find help

During my earliest years of motherhood when I was exhausted and overwhelmed, friends and family suggested that I look into hiring a mother's helper or a babysitter for a few hours a week so that I could catch my breath and re-energize. I rejected their advice and even felt like it was an indication that I was failing in some way as a mother instead of recognizing it for what it was: a smart way to take care of myself so that I could continue to be a good mom. Use the following resources to help you find a qualified sitter in your new community, if you are looking for a nanny for when you return to work, or if you feel like you are drowning in laundry and need some inexpensive, reliable help to keep you sane:

Sitter City
www.sittercity.com
Find a babysitter, nanny or other household help in your community with Sitter City. Sitters undergo background checks and customer reviews are readily available.

GoNannies
www.gonannies.com
Go Nannies is a web service that offers a relatively inexpensive membership plan for individuals looking for a nanny. Members can sign up for 45, 90 day and one year packages and can purchase additional detailed background checks on potential nannies including criminal and driving records, educational backgrounds and professional licensure.

Care
www.care.com
Care.com is a place for families to find childcare and pet sitters as well as experienced, inexpensive housekeepers to help with home maintenance. This is a website that definitely caters to people on a budget who need a little bit of extra help getting things done.

There is nothing wrong with asking for help when you need it. Since none of us are superheroes, it is also ok to need a helping hand. Hire a babysitter for a morning a week or pay a housekeeper to come in every other week to help you catch up on laundry or clean out the refrigerator if you can afford it. It is easy to get overwhelmed by raising children and being responsible for running things at home. A little bit of help can go a long way towards helping you recharge your batteries.

Nurture yourself

The responsibility of raising children can at times overshadow everything else going on in your life. It is easy to become so engulfed in the everyday tasks of taking care of the needs of our children that we can forget to look after ourselves. Even thinking about our own needs can feel uncomfortable sometimes. In order to thrive as a parent, it is essential to take care of yourself. You know what your needs are and what works for you when you feel the walls closing in on you. With this in mind, plan in advance for the possibility of having a bad day. This will allow you to nurture yourself and regain your balance. Here are some suggestions to help you lift your mood:

- ✓ Take a hot bath with a good book once the kids are asleep.

- ✓ Get out of the house with your children even if it means a trip to the park or a walk around the neighborhood. A change of scenery can work wonders.

- ✓ Keep a list of good friends on speed dial for that emergency pick-me-up.

- ✓ Dress up and put on make-up. If you're feeling droopy, looking good on the outside can lift your mood.

✓ Hire a babysitter for one morning a week and use the time to enjoy a cup of coffee, run, work out or simply catch up on your sleep.

Do what you can to take care of your own needs. You are worth it.

Chapter 6

The cost of parenthood

Measure wealth not by the things you have,
but by the things you have for which
you would not take money.
—Anonymous

I am transported into each weekend by my teenagers' outstretched hands.

"Mom, I need money for the movies."

"Can I go roller skating?"

"I need new shoes."

Before we had children, I had an idea that they were expensive. Now that I am fully immersed in motherhood I can say without a doubt that nearly every dollar we earn goes to our children in some way. Beyond the anticipated expenses of food and clothing are the healthcare extras like emergency room co-pays. There was the time when my oldest son broke his arm after falling off of his bike; the day after I had just paid for an expensive uniform for his summer marching band. My youngest daughter knocked a tooth out when she fell while playing with bubbles in the sink in the bathroom. After I stopped crying with her because I was so shocked and afraid, I was stunned into reality by the cost of the emergency dental appointment which included an MRI of the head to make sure that she had not damaged her brain in some way. The miscellaneous costs of raising children can range from the few dollars for the lost library book, to the eyebrow raising costs of tuition for private schools.

At every age and stage that our children have been through, I have been surprised by the additional costs that have cropped up. If I'm not ponying up for elementary school field trips, snacks, tuition for community education classes and birthday party gifts then I am digging through my purse for school lunches or middle school activity night. Raising children is expensive business.

We brought three children into the world during residency training. It might seem counterintuitive that we started our family during the training years when money was tight, but it felt like the right time for me to be able to be a stay-at-home mom. I knew that it would be difficult for me to work on my career while we were embarking on several cross-country moves. I was in good company. You might find it encouraging that not only are there couples starting their families during training, they are also managing to do it successfully despite the financial strain.

Get the most bang for your buck

It may not be possible to cut back on housing or food costs, but clothing and miscellaneous items like nursery furniture and toys are areas that definitely can be reined in.

Saving on children's clothes and furniture can be as straightforward as hunting for what you need at garage sales or going to your local second-hand shops. We bought our first crib for $20 at a garage sale. It was in perfect condition and it held up through an international move and two babies before we donated it. When our neighbor retired from teaching, she hosted a garage sale to get rid of all of her children's books. We stocked up on wonderful books for just pennies on the dollar. Buying children's clothing and toys second hand is a way that many families save money. If there are no nice second-hand stores near you, the web is also a notable place to find good deals. Beyond *eBay* and *Craig's List*, here are some other fun websites to try:

> **The Children's Wear Outlet**
> **www.thechildrenswearoutlet.com**
> The Children's Wear Outlet was started in 1966 and exists now as both a bricks and mortar and online retail store. Shop online or order a catalog to save up to 70% on brand name clothing and accessories.
>
> **Zulily**
> **www.zulily.com**
> Get savings on maternity clothes and products for children aged 0-8 by signing up with Zulily. Zulily advertises savings of up to 70% off of name brands for registered members.

Shopping the end of the season sales is another resourceful way to stock up on clothing items in new condition for the following year. Estimating children's sizes can sometimes be difficult, but the savings can be worth the risk.

Swap 'til you drop

They say the best things in life are free, and when it comes to things like kid's clothing, shoes, coats or furniture, that isn't far from the truth. During residency it is constructive to find creative ways to make your parenting dollar stretch as far as it can. If your infant has outgrown her *Bumbo* and *Exersaucer* you might be in the market for a tricycle or toddler bed. Before you have a garage sale, or drag your items down to the local resale shop, pick a Saturday and host a swap. Invite members from your playgroup, resident spouse alliance or friends with children to set up a garage swap.

What are the rules?

- ✓ All participants should set out items to exchange or give away to other swappers.

- ✓ The items should be cleaned up or washed and should be in a generally good condition.

- ✓ Exchanges can be made without worrying about ensuring an equal monetary value. If you get into a routine of having regular swaps, this eventually will even itself out as people need more or less things.

The swaps I participated in were organized like a garage sale, with clothing items on tables and the larger items nearby. After all contributors had set up their tables and laid out their items, everyone took about 15 minutes to walk around the tables to decide what items they wanted. There was a lot of chatter about who needed what, and we all found a way to help each other get the things that we needed.

Though a traditional swap can be a lot of fun, it is also a labor-intensive project. An alternative to the conventional swap is to host an *itemless* swap. Participants bring a list of items with or without pictures to share and the exchange or donation of items can happen later. This is a fun way to bring together a group of friends and celebrate the end of one post-graduate year.

Take advantage of any resources that will help you to save money while you are doing the hard work of raising your children. Use care when selecting pre-owned items like cribs or toys. If you can't verify that furniture meets current safety standards or that toy don't have loose parts that can be harmful, it is better to purchase the items new. Used car seats are generally not recommended. Safety has to come first.

Holidays and Birthdays

One of the most stressful parts of training from my perspective was the issue of gift-giving when it involved the children and extended family. As adults, my husband and I were able to understand that money was tight. We set a $10 gift limit for buying a small token for each other. It was always fun for us to hunt down the cheapest gift to exchange. Kids are a different issue altogether. They have very specific wishes when it comes to receiving gifts. Even now that we are finished with training, the holidays that involve gift giving continue to be a source of stress. Whether it is the latest *Wii* games or *American Girl* dolls, children's tastes in presents are usually expensive.

Do what you can to minimize your costs. Dollar stores are excellent sources of smaller gift items like coloring books, crayons, play-dough, puzzles, hair clips, dolls and a variety of other fun toys. Many of my stocking stuffers come from our local dollar store. I also like to stock up on items throughout the year. After Christmas, many stores have clearance items with discounts of up to 90%. Finding stocking stuffers and other holiday gifts throughout the year has become a fun challenge for me. I got into the habit of buying gifts throughout the year during residency, and I still do it.

For more expensive, big ticket items, watch for sales in advance of birthdays or holidays and consider second hand shops. We bought a *Gamecube* for half price at a local *GameStop* store one year. It was in perfect condition and our son never realized that it wasn't new.

As a final note, consider that homemade presents like t-shirts with children's handprints painted on them are an inexpensive way to give meaningful gifts to extended family.

Do it yourself

Everywhere you turn today as a parent it seems like there is pressure to involve young children in as many activities as possible. We are inundated with images of happy babies who are smarter because we have better prepared them to meet the challenges of today's society by signing them up for competitive preschool gymnastics or filling their minds with expensive educational DVD's.

Many companies offer *happy baby* classes that newborns can take part in. There are foreign language immersion classes for toddlers as well as music, fitness and school readiness programs. Your 18 month old isn't enrolled in Yoga? Oh, the shame. The pressure is on to enroll your children as soon as possible to ensure their spot at Harvard Medical School.

Lets' be honest. Many of these great programs just aren't in the budget for medical families during training. There is potential for real guilt and feelings of failure when we get caught up in feeling like we aren't doing enough for our children. These classes can be a great way for us to meet other moms and for our children to begin forming relationships with same-aged peers. They do have value. At the same time, medical training is generally a time of financial strain. Signing them up for expensive classes just might not be a financial reality. It wasn't for us. I agonized over the fact that we couldn't afford preschool, dance classes or expensive sports activities. We did the best that we could with the money that we had available. With time, I realized that we were meeting other families at the parks, libraries and play places. This didn't stop that gnawing fear that I was somehow cheating my children out of future happiness. Now that they are older, I realize that many of my fears were largely unfounded. My oldest son plays for his school's baseball team and my oldest daughter enjoys her dance classes. They have been able to find their way without immersion Chinese or competitive preschool gymnastics. We all have survived and are thriving.

The fact of the matter is that your children will learn to love reading if you read to them. Their language development will improve simply by talking and interacting with them. They can meet friends in the parks and at play groups. When they are little, putting on some fun children's music and dancing and singing with them will be enough. They don't need to be enrolled in formal art classes to turn them into Picasso. For my daughter, the walls in our rental townhome were the perfect canvas. It is ok to do it yourself when it comes to activities for small children.

There is a place for extracurricular activities. If you are interested in a *mom and me* class or have older children who want to get involved in dancing, music, karate, swimming, or other activities, check out your local *Community Education* office. Many school districts now offer youth enrichment programs in the afternoons and early evenings. You may be surprised to discover affordable classes in theater, foreign languages and science. If these things are not available in your area, keep in mind that you can provide enriching activities for your children that will be just as valuable. One of the women in our medical spouse alliance started a successful monthly book club for tween girls when her daughter was 11 to provide her with friendships and to stay involved. It was a huge success.

There are many resourceful ways to manage financially during residency when you are a parent. It's important to think outside of the box and be flexible about your expectations.

Chapter 7

Family building

The best things you can give children,
next to good habits, are good memories.
—Sydney J. Harris

Your alarm goes off at 6:00 a.m. and you hit the snooze button three times before finally crawling out of bed at 6:30 a.m. The rest of the morning is a blur of waking children and helping them to get ready for school. There are breakfasts to be made, lunches (that you swore you were going to take care of the night before) to pack, buses to catch and kids that need to be shuttled. If you are anything like me, you're ready for a nap by 9:00 a.m., but are so wired from the pot of coffee that you have infused into your tired veins that resting is not an option.

When you have kids your days are full and busy. Add residency training and a co-parent who is often missing-in-action to the mix and before you know it you are just putting one foot in front of the next to keep the household running. It can feel impossible to foster healthy family relationships when one parent is missing out on so much of the day-to-day family life and you are busy juggling everyone else's schedules. It is easy to get caught up in the daily to-do list and put off family building traditions. Energize yourself and your family by establishing new guidelines for family togetherness.

Become the family historian

Take pictures and keep family scrapbooks for the children to share with each other and with their hardworking parent. Include pictures of events that your spouse was unable to attend due to call schedules. If possible, let the children share the pictures and tell about the event themselves. It is important to try and minimize the negative effect of your spouse's absences when possible. Get a couple of snapshots of those post-call naps too and then keep it positive. It's all a part of the medical training experience too.

Visit mom or dad for a call night meal in the cafeteria, complete with a tour of the call room or children's waiting area. Take your camera and then capture those memories. Your children will thank you for it someday, and so will your spouse. In a slow time, you may be able to capture some family moments.

If you don't have time to sit down and sort through pictures to create a photo album, use one of the following websites to print out a photo book or photo flipbook from your digital photo files. The quality of the books is excellent. An additional bonus is that you can print out extra copies for the children and as gifts for grandparents.

Snapfish
www.snapfish.com
Effortlessly create albums and choose occasion-specific backgrounds.

Shutterfly
www.shutterfly.com
Shutterfly might be more expensive than Snapfish, but it has a wide variety of backgrounds to suit most occasions. They even boast a traditional "Martha Stewart" design.

Blurb
www.blurb.com
This is one of my all-time favorite photo printing websites. It is a good choice for larger scrapbooking projects. The Blurb software can be easily downloaded to your computer enabling you to work offline.

Along the same lines as creating photo albums is the suggestion to make videos of big events that your spouse can't attend. This is especially true for things like dance recitals, plays or baseball games. Make a big deal of sitting down to watch the re-run together as a family. The positive effects are two-fold: Your child gets to share the experience with their parent who was unable to be there, and your spouse has an opportunity to be a part of their children's lives on a deeper level than might otherwise be possible.

> **One True Media**
> **www.onetruemedia.com**
> One true media is a website that provides
> you with tools to create a photo montage
> with a musical background to
> commemorate special events. It serves as a
> video photo album. It is also possible to mix
> videos with the software as well.

One of the advantages of *One True Media* is that it is possible to put together a nice picture montage, and the videos are then available to purchase to give as gifts for family members and friends.

Create fun traditions

Pull yourselves out of the tedious day-to-day routine by coming up with new family traditions. During residency, the kids and I celebrated *Friday Family Fun Night,* where we did a craft activity like painting family t-shirts. We made Halloween decorations or watched a family movie. This was something that we did whether my husband was on call or was home and able to join us. This is a nice way to connect with your children at their level and also gives Dr. Mom or Dr. Dad a structured, pre-planned activity to engage in with the children when they are home and are able to join in. Stock up on inexpensive supplies at local craft shops when they have sales and then pull them out for craft nights. Not only will you be creating keepsakes to remember your children's early years, you will be providing them with happy memories. If you enjoy board games, dig out your *Chutes and Ladders, Monopoly, or Sorry* games and make family game nights a priority. Playing games is a great way to connect with your children and learn more about what is going on at school and with their friends while you have a good time.

As our family has grown and changed, our family fun night has been transformed as well. Family day is now Sunday and it usually involves popcorn and a fun movie in the family room. What is important is to take the time to do things together. Figure out a fun activity that you can all do as a family. Go on a family walk each evening around the neighborhood, plan a craft activity night or propose a weekly game or movie night. Do what you have to do to create fun, family-oriented entertainment.

If you are looking for some ideas to jump-start your family traditions stop by *Spoonful*.

> **Spoonful**
> **http://www.spoonful.com**
> Search this Disney sponsored website for cooking, craft and family game ideas.

Help your spouse step up to the plate

Yes, they are working long hours and are tired. It is reasonable to understand that they are exhausted and need time to recover. At the same time, they cannot be granted a free pass when it comes to parenting. One of the biggest mistakes that I made early in training was not insisting that my husband help bathe the kids or watch them so that I could have a few minutes to myself. I thought that I was helping him by giving him that down time. I also wanted to protect the children from his post-call grumpiness. He saw them so infrequently and I wanted their interactions to be positive. I had an idea in my mind of how things should be and I was not willing to give up the control that I thought that I had in building our family's life. In actuality, I was depriving them all of the opportunity to interact and relate with each other on their own terms. When my husband did finally have to step up to the parenting plate, he was easily overwhelmed and the kids were unhappy. My husband didn't know how to parent any more than I knew how to insert a central line. It took us a long time to undo the damage that had inadvertently been caused.

It is important to insist on some face time. This is my tough love stance. Your spouse played an equal role in creating your family and it is important to insist that they spend some one-on-one time with the child that does not involve falling asleep in front of the television.

Ask your spouse to help with specific parenting tasks, like bathing the children or tucking the kids into bed at least once a week. They could be involved in reading bedtime stories or driving to Saturday soccer practice when they aren't on call. Come up with a list of things with your spouse that they will enjoy doing with the kids and that will help them to get involved now. They might stumble and make mistakes, but it's important to step back and give them a chance to learn to parent.

Make dinner time count

Though busy call schedules often get in the way of a regular family meal, make the meals that you can share together a priority. Keep in the back of your mind that there is no *right* way to enjoy a family meal. I am guilty of wanting the Norman Rockwell moments. I used to imagine my children setting the table while I cooked, the delighted smiles over the entrée, and the happy and loving memories that we would be making. Fast forward to reality . . . when we are in the middle of a busy month, it can be hard to pull everyone to the table for a meal. After I bellow a final "and I'm serious" warning up the stairs, and the meal is getting cold, everyone settles into their places. There are invariably grumbles about the menu from someone, but often from more than one of the children. "Can I have cereal now?" is the most common question asked during dinner, followed by "do we have any peanut butter?". Cell phones vibrate from my teen-agers pockets and more often than not it feels like there is more arguing happening than anything else. It is definitely not the way that I imagined family meals, but sometimes I step back in the kitchen and listen as they argue about who got more noodles or what new song really *rocks*. They argue and disagree, but they are talking and sharing about their lives their way. As annoyed as I sometimes feel, I know that I will miss the chaos and noise someday.

Establish a regular family meeting

If you have children who are old enough to take part in some of the day-to-day planning that goes on in a family, institute a weekly family meeting. Use this as an opportunity to discuss family business like call schedules, school issues or plan play dates. This is a great way to catch up on what is going on in your children's lives and empower them during the training years. If the children feel like they are involved in the family planning, they may also be more invested in helping out around the house.

A word to the disheartened

It is easy to ask the question "why"? Why should I have to work so hard to keep my spouse actively engaged in our children's lives? Why can't they see what needs to be done or seek out those relationships with the children on their own? If you are asking yourself those questions, you aren't alone.

In my early years of being a mom, I was saddened by the fact that my husband wasn't around enough to play a larger role in the lives of our children. It sometimes felt like he was more of a visitor in our home than a husband and father. I initially put off establishing bedtime routines, dinnertime and family activities because I didn't want to do something that excluded him more from our lives. I realized that that I was cheating the kids out of fun memories. I began working at creating routines and traditions that we could enjoy together and when my husband was able to join us, having a set schedule helped him to join in and become involved. Instead of feeling awkward, he was able to pick up a paint brush and do crafts with us (or at least sit at the table and talk while we worked) and was able to help more with dinnertime or bedtime routines because he knew what to expect and what needed to be done.

Work hard to establish routines and traditions that include your spouse. It may not be fair that the burden of the child-rearing rests squarely on your shoulders. You may never hear a thank you for your hard work and investment in your family, but watching your family grow closer together will be its own reward.

Chapter 8

The family map

This is the precept by which I have lived:
Prepare for the worst; expect the best; and take what comes.
—Hannah Arendt.

The busy hum of the holiday season was fast approaching. I was 27 weeks pregnant with our fifth child and was actively working to balance our daily schedule of school and activities when I was unexpectedly hospitalized for health complications. My husband and parents were left to stumble through the children's schedules while I fielded stressed out phone calls from my hospital bed. I realized how unprepared my husband really was when it came to having to take over at home. Our division of labor had always required that I keep the household running smoothly so that he could see patients and take call. This unforeseen event caused a lot of confusion until we were able to come up with a detailed plan for getting everything accomplished.

Preparing for an unexpected event where you are suddenly unavailable to keep the household running smoothly is essential for busy families. This is particularly true if your spouse will have to shift from the now comfortable role of physician-in-training to mastering the family schedule. If you are placed on bed rest or become ill, it is important to have a backup plan in place to guide your spouse as well as family and friends who may have to step in and help out.

Another important reason to organize a family map is to keep your busy spouse informed about how things run in the house. The parent that is not actively involved in the daily care of the children just doesn't have the opportunity to learn the details of how the family works while they are busy taking call or preparing for exams. While they are occupied by the demands of residency, you are likely the one who is organizing the afterschool schedules and who knows which bedtime story is your preschooler's favorite. My husband makes a regular practice of browsing through my updated versions of our own family map. It makes him feel more comfortable with our daily routine and he has been able to rearrange his schedule to pitch in more now on really busy days for me.

A detailed family map will provide information about daily and weekly schedules, school-related information, children's food preferences, discipline techniques and family rules and emergency numbers.

Daily schedule

Don't take it for granted that your spouse knows the daily routine or how to organize the family agenda. Prepare a detailed list that includes the following information:

- ✓ *Wake-up time:* What time do the children need to get up each day in order to make it to school or daycare on time? My older daughter needs a minimum of an hour to primp and prepare herself for school. My 9 year old on the other hand can roll out of bed and into his clothes and catch the bus within 15 minutes of waking up if necessary. Do they wake up with their own alarm clocks or require help? What is your morning routine? List anything that might make the morning run more smoothly for your children in your absence.

✓ *Potty training schedule:* If you are potty training, be sure and include the potty routine so that it is not interrupted. List any favorite books that your child likes to read while sitting on the potty and provide information about pull-ups, big kid pants and how to handle accidents when they occur.

✓ *Meal times:* What time do the children usually have breakfast, lunch and dinner? Do they have a special afterschool or bedtime snack? Keep mealtime schedules handy and be sure to mention where snack items are hidden.

✓ *Bath time and Bedtime routines:* Be sure and spell out your daily routine for getting the kids cleaned up and tucked in. Do your little ones take a bath together? Mention any special body washes or shampoos that should be used as well as whether or not there are bath toys that the children enjoy playing with. This will make it much easier for your spouse to step into this new role in your absence.

Weekly schedule

Prepare a schedule of events and activities that you participate in on a weekly basis:

- ✓ When do the children have their Boy Scout meetings, dance classes and other extracurricular activities? Provide addresses and phone numbers so that anyone watching your children can get directions or cancel for the week.
- ✓ Supply any contact numbers for other parents who may be able to help carpool for a short period of time if necessary.

School-related information

As the primary caregiver, you are probably the parent who goes to school conferences, and talks with the teachers on a regular basis. I took it for granted that my husband shared my knowledge of the day-to-day school schedule, until one day half-way through the year when he had to drop off their lunches at school. He didn't know the names of the kids' teachers or even how to find the school office. Put together a list that includes:

- ✓ *School bus information:* If your children take the bus, what time do they need to go to the bus stop? Also, you may want to include information on where the bus stop is on your street as well as the bus number.
- ✓ *School start and end times*: Include names, addresses and telephone numbers of your children's schools.
- ✓ *Teacher names, room numbers and telephone numbers (if available).* Make it easy for caregivers to contact the teacher to fill them in and get any information about homework or snacks that need to be brought.

✓ *Homework routines:* If you have the kids do their homework after school, after dinner or before bedtime, be sure and make a note of it. In our house, dinner is at 6pm and homework time starts at 7pm. If the older children have more homework, they know to start earlier.

Food preferences

My older daughter is a vegetarian and my firstborn will not eat any food that is mixed together with anything else. The younger two boys will eat whatever is put in front of them as long as it doesn't have sauerkraut in it. The baby of the family will eat anything. This is important information. Picky eaters can be thrown completely off balance by a change in diet. Obviously, friends and family can't be expected to cater to the culinary whims of the children, but when choices are available, mealtimes will be easier if you put together a mealtime guide.

✓ *Note allergies or food sensitivities*: If anyone suffers from a food allergy, make a note of this and highlight it in yellow or red so that the information stands out and isn't overlooked.
✓ *Food preferences*: Indicate simple food items that the children enjoy, like spaghetti, macaroni and cheese or types of pizza that they would eat. This will take the pressure off of anyone having to cook for your family.

Discipline

Your spouse may be much more aware of the household rules and consequences, but this is a great thing to include in your family map in the event that a family member or sitter needs to care for the children. My daughter, for example is phased by nothing short of having her favorite computer game taken from her and time spent alone in her room. My oldest son, in contrast feels devastated if he has disappointed me. I can also sit and talk with him about behavioral issues. My daughter just gives me a wave of the hand, a toss of the hair and a "whatever". Each of our children responds better to different discipline techniques and preparing a good list of what works and what doesn't will make it much easier for someone having to step in and take over:

- ✓ What are the household rules?
- ✓ What consequences do you use when the rules are broken? Be child specific.

Emergency numbers

No family map would be complete without the standard listing of emergency contacts. This should include your pediatrician, dentist, orthodontist and other physicians who may be treating your children. Include any medications that they are taking as well as any other relevant medical information. This might consist of insurance information for the benefit of family members or friends who are watching your children as well as known allergies or other special healthcare issues.

Preparing for the unexpected event that you will be unable to care for your children for a short period of time may be an anxiety-provoking thought. Putting together a detailed map of your families' schedule will help to keep things running smoothly at home and will alleviate the pressure and concern that you ultimately will feel if you have to step out of your role as primary caregiver. Of course, you will want to keep all of this information in a place where it is easy to find. Attach it to the refrigerator, put it in your family planner, or place it in the kitchen drawer with your other important documents. It will help to provide your family with consistency in a time of stress which will allow you all to cope with the bump in the road.

Chapter 9

Moving with children

We do not remember days, we remember moments.
—Cesare Pavese

The hardest move I ever made followed my sophomore year in high school. My father had retired from the military the previous year and we had moved to what was supposed to be our forever and ever home in a small Midwestern town. For the first time in my life, I had a boyfriend. Each weekend we walked hand-in-hand through the cornfields and talked about our hopes and dreams for the future. Needless to say, the news of our impending move did not go over well. Mike was not just my first boyfriend. He was also my best friend. I was angry with my parents for an entire year after we moved.

As stressful as moving is for us as adults, it is important to remember that children can also feel distressed and overwhelmed by the changes taking place. It is essential not to let the children's needs for comfort and reassurance get buried beneath the chaos of planning and implementing the move.

Include children as much as possible in any aspects of the move that you can. Take pictures of the new house, neighborhood, or school and put them all together in a photo album for the children to keep and look through. This will help them begin to imagine what their new lives will be like so that they start approaching the changes from a place of excitement instead of fear.

The needs of your children will depend on their ages at the time of the move.

Preschoolers

Young children are especially susceptible to the stress that adults project. They are most able to get through transitions like moving when parents are positive about the changes and turn the experience into something positive. With three to five year olds, reading stories about moving and showing them pictures of their new town and home (if possible) can be great ways to ease the stress and help the adjustment to go more smoothly. In addition, it is helpful to pack when they

> **Books about Moving**
>
> *The Berenstain Bears Moving Day* by Stan and Jan Berenstain.
>
> *We're Moving* by Heather Maisner and Kristina Stephenson.
>
> *Moving House* by Anne Civardi, Michelle Bates and Stephen

are at preschool or to sign them up for a mother's day out program so that you can pack without interruption and then spend quality time with them later. Finally, preschoolers are old enough to pack up some of their things. Keep out some of their toys and allow them to pack these items right before the move.

This will help give them a sense of control and they will feel like they are helping.

Elementary School Children

School-aged children can play a much more active role in the moving process, but they are also likely to be more impacted by the impending changes than preschoolers. One effective way to lessen the stress that a young child feels is to offer them as much control over the experience as possible.

When my husband and I began house hunting near the end of fellowship, we had our children make a list of everything that they wanted in a house. The list looked something like this:

The house should be

- ○ White
- ○ Brown
- ○ Pink
- ○ Black
- ○ With stairs
- ○ With lots of stairs
- ○ With a backyard

The list was broad enough to include something for everyone. When our search was over, we made the big announcement. "We found the house you wanted. It is brown, has stairs and a backyard". We took pictures and printed them out before we arrived home. The children felt like they had selected the house for us. Ultimately, we all got what we wanted.

Tweens and Teens

Raising teenagers is stressful enough. Raising teenagers and moving with them? Easier said than done.

The good news is that your adolescent is old enough to help with things like cleaning out their rooms and getting rid of what they don't need or want. Oh wait, I'm sorry. Let me finish laughing. Did I just suggest that your adolescent would be able to help with cleaning and packing? In theory, this is probably true. The bad news is that it may take a lot of effort to enlist their help. The teenage years are a time of great change and your budding young adult may be resistant to lending a hand when it comes to having to leave their school and friends. My father-in-law used to say "little children, little problems; big children bigger problems". I dismissed his wisdom out of hand. Now I realize that I was the naïve one.

Giving your adolescents the opportunity to talk about their sadness and fear might relieve some of their concerns. My own mom was always good about letting me cry on her shoulders without dismissing my feelings. She let me be sad and angry and then talked to me about the positive changes that would be happening. I was eventually able to accept the move and start thinking about it in more positive terms.

Providing your adolescent with an outlet to talk about their feelings can be tricky. They may or may not want to talk or feel comfortable sharing their feelings with you. Their anger and disappointment might also be directed at you, which can make it difficult to step back and listen. It is hard to be supportive if your teenager is sullen and angry.

Another thing that can help is letting them take on as much responsibility for packing their rooms as they can (and are willing to do) so that they feel like they are in charge of their own belongings. In line with that is the suggestion to let older children pick out their new rooms when possible. We all like to feel like we have some control over our lives and giving your teen some say in the process will help them to manage their feelings of upheaval.

You are the expert on your children and you know what works best for you as a family. If giving them plenty of opportunities to open up is key, keep working on it. If they just need space to adjust and work through their feelings, it is ok to give them that too. As hard as it is, you will get through it and so will they. It will be ok.

Travel tips

My children have clocked many hours in the back of my VW van. Every summer, we set out on our annual *great adventure* together. We pick an exciting destination in Canada or across the country from where we live and then we embark on a week or two of bickering with each other and swearing that we will never take a long road trip together again. That being said, we always have the next year's destination picked out before we even make it home. I think the complaining is just part of our journey together. Of course, it could be born out of the many wrinkles that have cropped up during our travels: Camping in an area where there were more mosquitoes than oxygen molecules in the air; being trapped on a remote road with cows surrounding the van for over an hour . . . the list is endless. Our most interesting trip was to Regina Canada to prove once and for all to my teenage children that the capital city of Saskatchewan is pronounced re-jean-uh, not re-jine-a. I admit that it was an extreme way to teach this lesson. It had much more impact when I discovered that it is indeed re-jine-a. But, I digress . . .

Traveling is an exhausting and stressful experience. When children are along for the ride, it can become uncomfortable quickly unless you have put together a good travel plan.

Plan extra time

If you are making a big move with small children, give up the idea that you can drive through the night or travel 8 hours taking only quick bathroom breaks. Accepting this fact now will make your travel experience much less stressful. Ultimately, unless you want to be miserable, you will have to stop to let the kids stretch their legs and play. To be honest, my husband and I need the time to walk around and enjoy a break at least as much as the children do. We blame the extra time on them, but we are guilty too. If it's possible, research landmarks or fun diversions along the way ahead of time and plan to make your move a mini-vacation or educational experience for older children.

Pack travel toys

I used to be naïve in my approach to family travel. I imagined us driving down the road singing songs together and bonding as we passed from one mile marker to the next. Because of this firm desire to use travel time to really get to know my children better and to share the experience as a family, I banned all travel toys, mp3 players and DVDs. What happened, of course, is that spit balls hit me in the neck from the back seat, children cried, shoes were thrown, fake gas was passed, and I ended up stopping at a *GameStop* and buying the cheapest battery powered game systems I could find. I held out for several days, but take it from me: Entertain your kids with toys and games that are appropriate for taking along in the car. Invest in a few inexpensive toys that they will be able to use while traveling and keep once you have arrived at your new destination. Look for toys that have few loose pieces that can get lost in the car or those that don't make a mess:

- ✓ *Magnadoodle*
- ✓ *Light Bright* travel game
- ✓ *Vsmile* handheld learning game
- ✓ *Crayola Wonder* markers and coloring books

Older children might enjoy:

- ✓ Magnetic travel games (look at the dollar store)
- ✓ Gameboys
- ✓ MP3 players

Stock up on audio books and DVDs (if you have a player in your car) to pass the time. Avoid bringing books for the kids to read unless you are sure that they won't get carsick.

Pack snacks

Pack individual servings of granola bars, or cheerios. Keep the snacks handy for when your children get hungry between meals. Fill Sippy cups with water or bring bottles of water in a small cooler for when your kids are thirsty. We made the mistake of allowing colored juice boxes in our car. Our carpet was never the same.

Just to keep it real here, I have to add that when we travel, I also fill our travel basket with some sweet treats that they don't get that often. Granola bars are only interesting for so long. Single serving muffins, fruit snacks and crackers or cookies make the trip more fun for everyone. Once we go from not eating in the car to eating though, I mentally prepare myself for the fact that we will need to be cleaning it out thoroughly at the end of each day.

We pack healthy lunches, but we also make many unplanned stops at fast food restaurants. We eat on the go if there is no play area or we are pressed for time, which sometimes adds to the overall chaos and mess in our car.

Enjoy beginning this new stage of your life together as a family. Someday you will reminisce on these times. Turn your move into memories that you want to look back on.

Helping children adjust

Once you have arrived and started settling in, find activities for your kids to get involved in as soon as you can. One of the easiest ways to ensure a smooth transition is to give your children the opportunity to meet new friends while they continue to pursue their favorite pastimes. Look into Community Education programs, preschool classes or sports teams if you haven't already done so.

If you feel comfortable (and it is in line with your family values), help your child set up a *Facebook* account or email address and give them time to connect with old friends as they meet new ones. Though moving can be difficult, children are resilient and often adjust well in a short period of time.

I survived my moves during high school and the trauma of leaving my first boyfriend behind. I went on to college, married my soul mate and began raising a family. Despite the fact that our lives have changed through the years, each Christmas Mike and I still try to keep in touch. We have both moved on with our lives, but we still take the time to keep up with each other when we can.

Part Three
Education and Career

Ambition means longing and striving to attain some purpose.
Therefore, there are as many brands of ambition as
there are human aspirations.
—B.C. Forbe

This year's Medicine Department Christmas party invitation arrived like it does every year . . . two weeks before the party, with suggestions for hors d'oeuvres or desserts that we should bring, and addressed to Dr. Thomas Math, MD and Uristan.

Uristan?

Small country in the Middle East? My relative calm about this now is a testament to how much I have grown since my husband began training. After years of fighting to be seen as my husband's equal and to be known as someone other than his wife, I decided to embrace *Uristan* as my inner exotic warrior woman. I spent the first part of my marriage as an army of one trying to forge my own professional identity. It took me years to accept that my own career would need to take a back seat and that I might always be *the doctor's wife*, no matter what my profession. This has freed me to choose a direction for my life and focus on my own happiness instead of recognition from my husband's peers.

If you are gainfully employed, 100% certain about your career direction and are currently satisfied with your professional life, this section is not for you. You are one of the lucky few who have already managed to find the balance between your career goals and the rigors of medical training.

If, on the other hand, you have been caught recently looking in the mirror uttering the words "who am I?", "I just want to carve out a tiny piece of my life that is just for me?" or if you have just finished another search under sofa cushions, in old purses and beneath the car seats and have emerged triumphantly with enough money to buy that cappuccino, these next chapters may be helpful to you.

My own medical training journey had been punctuated at times by all of these themes. I have gone from being a hopeful pre-med myself to being an exuberant and proud stay-at-home mom, to climbing the walls and regularly sorting and ironing baby clothes to take in to the second hand shops. OK, so maybe I didn't actually iron the clothes . . . but I did think about ironing them. Perhaps it is simply an attempt at self-protection here, but I think that going through these periods of doubt is a normal part of going through the changes that are a regular part of the medical training process, if not life itself. Moves for medical training and the all-encompassing focus on the physician interfere with the careers of many medical spouses.

Chapter 10

Work from home

A wise man will make more opportunities than he finds.
—Francis Bacon

The boxes are unpacked and the dust has settled from your move (or at least the dust bunnies are hiding safely under the sofa). Now that your spouse has taken the next step in their own career, you may be sitting at home wondering what has become of your professional life. This is a considerable issue for many people who have had to make considerable professional sacrifices in order to move for training. Our identities are often wrapped up (at least partly) in our careers. It is a very difficult and selfless act to support someone else's career when it means that your own dreams take a back seat.

If money is tight, the issue of working may be less about personal fulfillment and more about finding a way to generate a second income and survive financially. This can be more complicated if a move for training means that opportunities to work in your field are more limited. Working from home can be a practical solution for supplementing the household income and finding career satisfaction.

Is Telecommuting for you?

Do you have a noisy dog that barks if a leaf blows off of the neighbor's tree? Are your toddlers climbing on your chair and spilling coffee on your keyboard when you try and check your email? The level of noise and your ability to have several uninterrupted hours during the day to work professionally might directly affect your ability to be successful working from home.

Employers are looking for skilled people who can meet deadlines and at times talk with clients over the phone. To telecommute successfully, you will ideally need to have your own office space (or at least a nook in your home to store your work-related materials that is away from the *Crayola* markers and new kitten) to work at during office hours.

Things to consider:

Uninterrupted time to complete job-related tasks

If you have small children, you may need to hire a babysitter to take care of the children's needs if you are working in a position that demands your undivided attention. At the same time, if you choose a job with flexible hours, you may have no problem sitting down to work once the children are in bed.

A computer with high speed internet access

A desktop can provide you with a stable and potentially more powerful office computer. Laptops offer more flexibility. The type of computer that you need will depend upon the job you are doing and your need to be portable.

Working from home does require a level of dedication and autonomy that can be intimidating. The ability to stay on task in the home environment requires self-discipline, organization and self-direction. If, like me, you are easily distracted by the dirty dishes in the sink or the unwashed clothes exploding from the laundry room, working from home may be a less realistic option for you.

Find your match

Generally speaking, there are two categories of work at home jobs. There are opportunities to continue working in traditional positions from a home office that appeal to professionals who are looking to maintain their current skills and income. This might include telecommuting opportunities for accountants, attorneys, educators, photographers and even personal assistants. The potential for professionals to successfully work from home has become well-recognized by companies over the last several years. Many employers are now willing to give employees the opportunity to move from the more traditional office setting to a telecommuting arrangement.

Before moving on for residency or fellowship, it is definitely worthwhile to approach your employer and offer them the opportunity to let you continue your work for them as a telecommuter. Prepare a formal proposal to:

1. Outline the job that you could continue to do for them.

2. Highlight the benefits to them of keeping you on; including not having to retrain a new employee and being the beneficiary of your consistent, high quality work.

If telecommuting from your current job is not an option, there are many legitimate companies that actively look for skilled professionals that will allow you to work from home and contribute to the family income.

It is important to look for a job that fits both your interests, skills and your family situation. A position in data entry might be a bad fit if you are not a skilled typist. As interesting as a job as a legal transcriptionist might be, without the appropriate training, working in the field would be impractical. Obviously, it would be difficult to work in telemarketing if you have young children that could interrupt a phone call. Spend some time assessing your skills, educational background, interests and family situation. This will help you to determine what type of work-at-home job is the best fit for your particular needs.

There are many more job listings and telecommuting job search engines available online. Beware of any website that requires you to register and pay to read job listings. Most legitimate companies provide information about job openings at no cost to you.

An alternative to the traditional office job is the growing field of party professions. Direct sales can appeal to at home parents or individuals with an interest in sales and a particular niche market. If you have an interest in educational toys, kitchen products, cooking, jewelry, scrapbooking or other specific areas, there is probably a company that will allow you to build your own business as an independent sales consultant. Many consultants enjoy earning extra money while they meet new people and sell a product that they feel passionate about. The downside is that many of these companies require you to pay for an initial sales package to sign on as a consultant, and inventory purchasing requirements can eat into your profits. For a complete listing of reputable direct sales companies, visit the **Direct Selling Association** website.

Direct Selling Association
www.dsa.org
The Direct Selling Association is the national trade association for businesses that provide direct sales products to consumers. They promote ethical business practices that

If it sounds too good to be true . . .

Legitimate telecommuting opportunities are available for serious applicants that would like to have the chance to earn part-time or full-time wages while enjoying the flexibility of working from home. Consider any job carefully before making a commitment. If a job requires that you pay money for more information, asks that you pay fees upfront for any parts to assemble or just sounds too good to be true, walk away before you end up losing money.

Chapter 11

Explore a new path

We Work to become, not to acquire.
—Elbert Hubbard

One of the most notable career success stories that I remember from residency involved the male spouse of a surgery resident. He had a background in accounting but was unable to find employment in his field. After months of frustration, he made the decision to focus his talents in a new direction. Instead of risking several years of unemployment, he embarked on a career in real estate. Though he anticipated that this would be a temporary change, he discovered a passion for this new direction and very successful. After his wife finished with residency and they had moved on to life post training, his new real estate business flourished. If you are standing at a fork in the road because there are no openings for someone with your professional background, it might be time to spread your wings and make a temporary career change.

Investigate your interests

When you were in college, did a certain subject outside of your major spark your interest? Have you always seen yourself in a different profession, but feel like you are already committed to your current direction because of the time that you have invested? The training years can provide you with an outlet to explore your own professional interests and may present you with new opportunities to find your calling. Evaluate your previous job experiences. Consider each position that you have held individually:

✓ What did you enjoy about the job?

✓ What did you dislike?

Take an inventory of your personal and professional interests to look beyond your current occupation. Start by visualizing your dream job. Did you always want to own a bookstore or imagine starting your own restaurant? Try your dreams on for size and see if they are something that you can realistically begin to work towards. If you do not have a clear idea of what direction you would like to take, evaluate the subjects of interest to you and some of the careers that they might lead towards.

Assess your skills

Do you have a knack for repairing electrical equipment? Have you always been gifted when it comes to working with numbers? If you know a foreign language, can build a website or have the skills necessary to set up a network database, don't underestimate the potential value of these skills in the workplace. Review your hobbies and talents that you aren't necessarily using in your occupation and consider how these skills might transfer to a new job. Could you teach Spanish through your local Community Ed program? Does starting up a web design business sound enticing? Evaluate your abilities and look for creative, outside-the-box applications.

Assess your weaknesses

Ouch. I know. No one likes to give much thought to areas where they don't excel. My own personal list is long and spending too much time focusing on the negatives is unlikely to be very productive. That being said, recognizing your weaknesses can give you opportunities for growth or point you in the direction of careers that you are better suited for.

I was a terrible fit in the science lab because of my talkative nature. I enjoyed the process of research, but my first priority was always to find out how everyone was doing. I was as interested in hearing about the undergraduate students' applications for graduate school as I was in finding out whether or not my cell cultures had grown. As a result, the lab really just wasn't the right work environment for me, even though I wanted for it to be. Though I had never before considered teaching as a career, I later discovered that it was something I excelled at and more importantly, that I enjoyed.

Can your weakness be turned into a strength? Does your perfectionism make you a good fit for a field where attention to detail is important? Recognizing areas that you might consider weaknesses can help you to sell yourself better professionally or refocus your attention on a career more in line with your personal strengths.

What is your interpersonal style?

Your personality can play an important role in finding the right career for you. Listen to your instincts about your personality traits and how they fit into your most recent job experiences. You may be able to fine-tune your career to meet your interpersonal style.

Interpersonal Skills Assessment

I am:
- ○ Artistic
- ○ Cheerful
- ○ Creative confident
- ○ Independent
- ○ Outgoing
- ○ Nurturing
- ○ Patient

- ○ Practical
- ○ Quiet
- ○ Self-
- ○Shy
- ○Tenacious
- ○_____
- ○_____

If you are independent and outgoing, a career in business or management might be a good fit for you. If you are blessed with patience and a nurturing personality, a career in nursing, teaching or psychology might bring you the most happiness.

Identifying your own interpersonal style can help you to decide on a rewarding direction for your own career.

Consider your current educational background

Your educational background and training can be important tools to helping you find a new direction in your career. It isn't necessary to stay within the field that you have trained, so use your education as a guide and let it work to your advantage. If you have a degree in psychology, but are interested in working in business, you may be able to market your degree as being an additional benefit for working in the business world.

Evaluate your education and assess the skills that previous training and job experience has provided you with.

What is your background?

Do you have a high school diploma? Have you taken college classes or completed a degree program? Did you attend a technical program or get hands on experience working as an apprentice? Evaluate your academic and work experience.

What are your skills?

What applicable skills did your education provide you with? This is a particularly important question if you are hoping to use your current education to switch directions or change fields altogether.

Take action

Once you have assessed your interests, and skill sets, make a decision about what your next step should be and take action. If you have decided to reinvent your career, take the time to investigate any steps you will need to take to set your new plan in motion. Rework your résumé, send out applications, look for volunteer work to help you gain new experiences, or go back to school. Keep your future goals in mind as you make changes in your professional life.

If you are concerned about being able to step back into your traditional career role at a later time, it might be important to choose a route that is parallel to your previous positions but offers you the option of expanding your skills. Reflect on your short and long term career goals to start narrowing down your options. If you aspire to an executive position in the future, taking a job at the local coffee shop is clearly a step in the wrong direction. Accepting a position at a local halfway house may add to your skills as a social worker when you return to counseling work.

Chapter 12

Volunteer

Extending your hand is extending yourself.
—Rod McKuen

When my husband finished fellowship we were both eager to move and start our life post-training. We agreed that I would go back to staying at home for at least the first year while we all transitioned yet again. I had assumed that when I was ready to go to work that opportunities would be readily available. What I had not calculated was that I had been out of the workforce for long enough that my skills were a bit . . . rusty. To top it off, I wasn't feeling as confident about my abilities and the job prospects were lousy. It felt like the doors were slamming shut around me. I decided to offer to work as a volunteer for a year at one of the nearby universities. The experience that I gained was invaluable. I was given the opportunity to teach and work with people in a completely different manner and setting than I had before. This definitely took me out of my comfort zone but I learned new skills and enjoyed the experience. Ultimately, my volunteer work also evolved into a paid position.

In an ideal world, after moving for medical school, residency or fellowship, the job of our dreams would fall into place. For many people though, the reality of the training years can mean accepting that job opportunities may be less than ideal. If you are considering volunteering, there are several ways to go about finding a position that will meet your needs.

Define what you want

What do you hope to gain from your volunteer experience? Does this seem like a good time in your life to give back to others and help make a difference in your community? Are you looking to maintain your skills or learn new ones while helping others? Maybe you are interested in trying out a new professional field altogether. Take the time to identify your strengths and weaknesses as well as your career interests and motivations. Volunteering may be a rewarding way to gain new skills and direction in your own career.

Evaluate where you are professionally and reassess your five year goals. Be sure and consider what it is that you have to offer and the length of time that you are willing to volunteer. You may have a particular business or organization in mind. If not, the web is another avenue to help you find a good match:

Volunteer Match
www.volunteermatch.org
Volunteer match can help you find local volunteer opportunities. Their search engine allows you to enter how far you are willing to travel as well as the areas of interest to you. It then provides you with a list of potential volunteer positions in your area.

Contact the organization personally

Once you have narrowed down your search to specific organizations, visit their websites to find out as much information as you can about their philosophies, business activities and their volunteer opportunities. If you are interested in volunteering for a company that does not advertise volunteer positions, contact them anyway. They may be willing to accept your offer to help. Research the organization or company to consider where you could offer the most help or learn the skills that you are hoping to acquire. Call and set up an appointment to talk with the individual in charge of volunteer positions or the director of human resources. emailing or mailing a resume should be done only after you have already spoken with someone about available opportunities.

Be prepared to discuss your previous positions, your reasons for volunteering and how you feel that you could benefit them. Consider it a practice job interview. Volunteering is an opportunity to learn new skills and explore your talents and interests. Ultimately it can be an invaluable investment in your future career by providing you with new skills, resources, professional contacts and references.

Utilize your time

Volunteer work is an innovative way to open yourself up to new experiences and to acquire skills that can benefit you professionally for years to come. Take advantage of the variety of projects available in your new position, even if they fall outside of the realm of what you thought you wanted to do. Recognize this as a low-stress way to learn how to give presentations, meet with clients or even make a good cup of cappuccino.

Keep in mind that not only are you are giving yourself the opportunity to explore change and hone new skills, you are also presenting yourself in a professional environment. Show up for work on time, just as you would if this was a paid position. Your professionalism will be rewarded later when you ask for a letter of reference for your next paid position.

Update your CV

This probably seems like a no-brainer. Don't forget to update your CV before you leave your volunteer position. It is much easier to write down contact information and supervisors while you are still in the work environment. Once you move on for residency, fellowship or an attending position, the details can get lost in the shuffle and will take more energy to reconstruct.

Chapter 13

Hit the books

Education is not the filling of a pail, but the lighting of a fire.
—William Butler Yeats

When my husband began residency in the United States, I had been a full-time stay-at-home-mom for almost two years. I hadn't intended to go back to school, but within months of the onset of internship year I found myself feeling desperate for some type of stimulation beyond the daily challenges of parenting. My husband's consistent absences were taking their toll on me and I was looking for something to do to carve out a piece of our lives that was just about me. I already had my bachelor's degree in the social sciences and so I decided to revisit a field that had been of interest to me in college: Biology. I enrolled as a second degree student for the minimum number of credit hours that I needed to qualify for financial aid. I didn't know what I expected to achieve by going back to school, but I was grateful for the outlet for myself and for the opportunity to change the direction of my career.

Each semester was both a challenge and an adventure. I chose classes that interested me. I studied in the McDonald's play areas or when we were out at the park. Some semesters were raving successes and others were disappointing, but I continued because my studies seemed to anchor me to myself. I was surprised to discover a real passion for biology. By the end of my husband's fellowship, I had earned my MS in molecular biology. When I began taking classes it never occurred to me that my life would take the direction that it has and yet if I could go back in time now, I wouldn't change a thing.

People choose to go back to school for a variety of reasons. They may be looking for career advancement, continuing education opportunities or just a new challenge. The career limbo of the medical training years can be an opportunity for you to do some soul searching about your own career aspirations and reinvent yourself. Whether you already have a college degree under your belt or have never contemplated taking a college course, it is possible to use this time to add to your current qualifications or switch directions altogether.

Pick a major

If you have a good idea of the path that you would like to take and have selected a major, you are ahead of the game. With so many choices available, it can be difficult to narrow down your options. When considering college majors, reflect on two main factors:

1. Your genuine interest for the subject matter.

2. Marketability of the degree after graduation.

It's important that whatever you choose to study is something that you will enjoy and have a desire to learn more about. You don't want to spend several years dreading class only to realize that the jobs you can get involve skills that just aren't of interest to you. By the same token, if you choose a major based purely on your passion for a subject and don't combine it with practical skills, you may be investing in a very expensive piece of paper. Find a balance between your interests and what is marketable. Before you waste a lot of time searching for career aptitude quizzes online and discover that you have to register with your email and your home address in order to review the results, recognize that you already know who you are and where your interests and abilities lie. Create a list of subject areas of interest to you and fields that you might be interested in studying. If you need help, pick up a handbook from your local university to browse through their majors or explore your options online.

College Board
www.collegeboard.com/csearch/
majors_careers/profiles
Browse through a listing of college majors or career interests. College Board has created a considerable list of career options complete with detailed information about the profession, the outlook for future employment and potential compensation.

CareerOneStop
www.careeronestop.com
Career One Stop is a website sponsored by the US Dept. of Labor. Explore careers, education and salaries and also get help with resumes and interviewing. Career One Stop even helps you plan your job search and links to state and local job banks.

If you continue to feel uncertain about which career direction to move towards, make an appointment with your local university counseling center to set up an interview for aptitude testing.

Explore the local colleges or universities in your area

Start your search in your local yellow pages or on the web. Most colleges and universities now have websites where you can browse through a listing of degree programs, courses and their costs as well as financial aid programs. Many colleges even allow you to apply for admission online. If you are unsure of how to begin your web search, the following websites are a good jumping off point:

AASCU
www.aascu.org
The American Association of State Colleges and Universities website provides a listing of colleges and universities by state.

AACC
www.aacc.nche.edu
The American Association of Community Colleges has an interactive community college locator that allows you to click on a US Map to find local colleges. In addition, free access to *Community College Times*, the online AAAC journal provides interesting articles relevant to students and educators.

Some important factors for you to consider when going back to school include:

✓ *Location:* Is the school located within a 10-20 mile radius from your home or will a longer commute be necessary?

✓ *Cost:* What is fee for one credit hour? If there are several local colleges or universities, it is worth your while to compare the costs and weigh the benefits of each school carefully.

✓ *Flexibility:* Does the school offer evening or weekend classes? Are there multiple sections available for each class, or does a smaller student body mean less flexibility to fit your classes into your own schedule?

Another significant issue to consider is the length of time that you and your spouse will be in one location for residency and the time that you will need to complete a degree program. If your spouse is doing a three year Emergency Medicine residency and you will need four years to complete a bachelor's degree, consider taking only courses that will transfer to another school when you move or focus on getting your associates degree. Don't set unrealistic goals for yourself. If you have children and your husband is a resident, you may not be successful taking 18 credits per semester unless you have a nanny . . . and maybe a personal chef and housekeeper. Your family's needs are unique and so you are the best judge about what is realistic or doable for you.

Financing your education

It is undeniable that college is an expensive investment in your future. With tuition rates fluctuating between $100 and $1500 per semester hour, the goal of going to school can feel unattainable. It is possible to return to college during residency. My husband and I were initially very skeptical about the possibility of financing my degree. We were barely getting by each month and it would have been impossible for us to come up with the tuition on our own. The good news is that there are a variety of loan and scholarship programs available to help you. They are relatively easy to get and provide for tuition and additional cost-of-living expenses. The bad news is that once you take out the money, you will eventually have to pay it back. The days of locking in a 3% interest rate for your Stafford loans are long gone, so it is important to think long and hard about how much debt you are really willing to repay.

Federal loans

Uncle Sam is often willing to lend a hand when it comes to financing college. Applying for federal Stafford loans has also never been easier. A visit to the Free Application for Federal Student Aid (FAFSA) website will allow you to find out all information about the subsidized and unsubsidized loan options, including the amounts you are eligible for and the ability to apply for the loans directly online.

FAFSA
www.fafsa.ed.gov
The application deadline for each academic year is usually June 30. This varies by state. Detailed information is provided online. To apply for financial aid through the website, you will need your:

- ✓ Social Security
- ✓ Driver's
- ✓ W-2
- ✓ Bank and mortgage
- ✓ Signature PIN (apply online)

Private loans

If applying for federal loans hasn't sufficiently scared you away from borrowing money, and you are coming up short in the dollar signs department, there is an endless supply of companies eagerly awaiting your application for private student loans. These loans are dependent on your credit score and some may require a co-signer if you do not have a current source of income or if your credit is less than perfect.

> **Access Group**
> **www.accessgroup.org**
> Access Group has a loan finder search option which lets you find the best loan to fit your needs. They also fun Stafford Loans at rates as low as 6.55%.
>
> **Collegiate Student Loans**
> **www.collegiatestudentloans.com**
> Collegiate Loans advertises a choice loan that allows you to choose a fixed or variable rate product. As with all private loans, rates are subject to your credit history.
>
> **CitiAssist**
> **www.citiassist.com**
> CitiAssist boasts that they offer online applicants with a credit response in 3 minutes. They don't require a minimum loan amount and defer payments until after graduation.

A word of caution: Private lenders like to give loans because they can earn a lot of money at your expense. My private loans were a huge thorn in my side for years. Despite a relatively low interest rate, by the time I finally paid off the balance, I had paid the loan amount plus a great deal more. Think carefully about adding private student loan lenders to the list of people you owe.

Scholarships

The best money that you can find to help you to finance your college education is money that is given to you for skills, aptitudes or talents. Applying for scholarships is a process that can involve submitting transcripts or essays, securing letters of recommendation, presenting artistic portfolios or performing on a musical instrument. To find more information about available scholarships, contact your school's financial aid office and visit the following scholarship search engines.

> **Fastweb**
> **www.fastweb.com**
> Fastweb has a large database of scholarships. After a free registration process, scholarships are automatically matched to your profile summary.
>
> **Scholarships.com**
> **www.scholarships.com**
> scholarships.com has a searchable database of more than 2.7 million scholarships and grants.

The types of scholarships available are as varied as the individuals applying for them. Taking the time to research grants and free financial awards will pay off in the end.

Chapter 14

Study in your pajamas

Success isn't a result of spontaneous combustion.
You must set yourself on fire.
—Arnold H. Glasow

The internet has taken education to an all new level of accessibility. It doesn't matter where you live or what you are interested in studying. Chances are, with a little bit of research, you can find the course or degree program that is right for you and that you can embark on while wearing your pajamas and your favorite slippers.

When I went back to school to get my master's degree, I really struggled to find on-campus classes that fit into my schedule, allowed me to pursue my education and be available to my children at the same time. I was very fortunate that the director of my graduate program encouraged me to look into distance learning options.

The choices today are astonishing. You can earn your PharmD online at Creighton University, study marine biology at Nova Southeastern and take courses in chemistry, math, psychology or theology at a wide variety of accredited universities with the click of a mouse. The list of options is seemingly endless. Ohio State University even offers a distance learning option for the first two years of medical school.

Is distance learning right for me?

Deciding to take courses online should be made with your personality and individual learning style in mind. Having a computer with internet access is a technical requirement that is easy to accomplish. Being self-motivated and possessing the ability to work independently may be an entirely different story. Keeping up with lectures and assignments when you aren't sitting in a classroom a few days a week can be challenging.

Do you need the structure of a classroom to force you to keep up with required readings? Are you self-directed or does meeting regularly with an instructor and classmates help you to maintain your focus? There is no right or wrong answer to these questions. It is very easy to say "I'll read that chapter tomorrow". Do some soul-searching about what type of learning style works better for you.

For me, the answers are dependent on the subjects that I'm studying. I am pretty good about being self-directed when the course involves something I'm interested in and that I excel at. Unfortunately, with subjects that I find more challenging, like anything chemistry or physics related, interactive chat sessions or professor emails just don't do it for me. In those situations, I need the classroom environment to motivate me and to help propel me forward.

Finding a distance learning course or program

Once you have tried on the idea of distance learning and have decided to take a course or work towards a degree, finding the right university will be the next challenge. Look at your local universities and at schools that are in your state of residence first. You don't want to pay out-of-state tuition if you can avoid it. Also, enrolling in a nearby university still gives you the option to take on-campus classes or to meet with professors in person if you need some extra help. You can find out the distance learning options available at area schools simply by going to their website and searching for their distance learning department. Most colleges and universities now have expansive lists of courses available online.

> **Petersons**
> **www.petersons.com**
> Fastweb has a large database of degree programs and courses that can be accomplished through distance learning.
>
> **ELearners.com**
> **www.elearners.com**
> elearners provides a wealth of information about online courses and programs. Their searchable database contains only accredited programs. They offer a variety of articles about distance learning as well as blogs and forums.

In addition to local searches, it is possible to find courses using some of the online search engines. These are great resources that can act as a good starting point, but if you are interested in a specific university, a visit to their website is the best way to find out what they offer.

Look for several different programs or classes and then narrow your search down by evaluating the cost of each class as well as the mode of instruction. Above all else, look for courses that have interactive office hours, lectures to download using streaming audio and video as well as group assignments and a well-organized syllabus. Course delivery is variable and it would be disappointing to invest a lot of money in a class that involved you simply reading a chapter and taking an exam. There are many classes set up that imitate a real classroom. If information about the class is not readily available, don't be shy about emailing the professor to ask questions about the format.

Accreditation

Before you make a final decision about taking classes at an institution, you will need to evaluate its accreditation. Obviously, if you are enrolling in an extension program through Harvard University, there is no question about the school's recognition as a reputable degree granting institution. If, however, you have found a school that you aren't familiar with, the accreditation will need to be verified for both the school and the program that you are interested in.

Look for information that confirms that a given school is accredited by a legitimate accrediting agency. **The Council for Higher Education Accreditation** provides a searchable database of accredited schools at their website.

Council for Higher Education Accreditation (CHEA) www.chea.org/search
The CHEA lists schools that have undergone rigorous accrediting procedures to insure quality.

Some common legitimate accrediting agencies include:

North Central Association of Colleges and Schools

Middle States Association of Colleges and Schools

Northwest Commission on Colleges and Universities

Southern Association of Colleges and Schools

Research the accreditation of any prospective program carefully before making your final decisions.

Beyond institutional accreditation, if you are looking at studying for a degree that also requires graduation from a program accredited by a particular organization for licensure, do your research and be sure that the institution you are applying to is approved by the appropriate licensing board. For example, Clinical Psychology graduate programs require accreditation by the American Psychological Association. Graduating from an unaccredited program may affect your ability to become licensed or practice.

There are still schools out there that offer unaccredited degrees for a minimum amount of effort, life experience or payment. If it sounds too good to be true, it is. There is no easy way to get a genuine college degree.

Financial aid

Students in most distance learning programs are eligible for the same financial aid packages as students in traditional on-campus programs. You may need to contact the college's financial aid office for help in applying for the various aid programs, but eligibility for federal Stafford loans and many private loans is not usually impacted by the method of delivery of the courses you are taking.

Part Four
Financial Survival

Measure wealth not by the things you have,
but by the things you have for which
you would not take money.
—Anonymous

As I write this, the *Autumn 2010 Survey of Resident/Fellow Stipends and Benefits* for residents has been released by the Association of American Medical Colleges (http://www.aamc. org). The average resident salaries for post graduate training years one through eight are found in Table 1.

Table 1: Average Resident/Fellow Salaries for 2010

Post Graduate Training Year (PGY)	Mean Salary in US Dollars
Pgy-1	48,460
Pgy-2	50,361
Pgy-3	54,541
Pgy-4	56,670
Pgy-5	50,829
Pgy-6	58,845
Pgy-7	60,955
Pgy-8	63,837

https://www.aamc.org/download/158738/data/2010_stipend_report.pdf

At first glance, these salaries seem to be reasonable, and they are if you consider that there are many families struggling to survive on much less. Toss in the fact that the average resident is working 80 + hours a week for a wage of less than $10/hour before taxes and are unlikely to be contributing to a retirement account for the future. Consider also that the average resident left medical school in 2010 with $148,222 in debt from a public institution and $172,422 in debt from a private institution (American Association of Medical Colleges). To further complicate matters, although 14% of medical students graduated with no debt, a staggering 43% entered residency with over $200,000 in debt (American Association of Medical Colleges). When put into context, the salaries no longer reflect the cost and effort required to pay back loans and maintain the long work hours.

All of that being said, when my husband was in his first year of training (PGY-1), his starting salary was $32,000. We thought this was a huge amount of money and couldn't understand why people were having trouble getting by until we began to struggle ourselves. We had accumulated a great deal of consumer debt paying for USMLE exams, interviews for residency and the associated moving costs. After we paid our rent, electricity, car payment on the one car that we owned, and bought groceries, there was very little left over. We definitely were not setting money aside for retirement, life insurance or to accumulate an emergency savings fund. Some months, we found ourselves paying for diapers or gas for the car with the credit card. We rationalized this by recognizing that eventually he would earn an attending salary and we would be able to afford to pay our debt off. The end result for us was an overwhelming consumer debt that grew larger every month of residency.

It is easy to fall into the *we'll pay it back later* trap, but it is very painful financially to crawl out of that hole. It took us nearly four years post-training to simply have some breathing room. Actually, for the first two years after my husband finished fellowship, we had lawn chairs for furniture in our living room.

Chapter 15

Living on a budget

Torture numbers, and they'll confess to anything.
—Gregg Easterbrook

Generally speaking, money is a taboo topic. My friends and I can talk about our labor and delivery experiences, political ideals or religious differences. Toss in finances and the conversation screeches to a halt. Financial health is as important of a topic as physical and emotional health, but it continues to remain socially unacceptable to discuss. My husband and I have struggled throughout our marriage to manage our finances and learn to budget. We have learned by making mistakes and the pain of trying to correct them. Our first financial *aha* experience came late one evening at the checkout of the local grocery store during fellowship. After paying for a costly car repair, we realized that we would have to pay for groceries with our credit card. As the clerk ran our card through the register, it immediately became apparent that there was a problem. I'll spare you the embarrassing details where I rummaged through my purse and my husband mentally calculated our available credit on the card. Forget the part where we argued back and forth with each other in German and I cried all the way to the car. We left the grocery store that evening without any groceries, and that was the painful bottom line.

That was the moment that we knew that things would have to change. Getting our finances under control has been a long and difficult process, because by the time we started to work on it a lot of the damage had already been done. Preserving financial control in the midst of medical training can be difficult, particularly if only one partner is working. With extra planning and creative problem-solving, financial survival can be much less challenging.

Prepare a budget

I'm not sure why the idea of coming up with a monthly budget used to fill me with an overwhelming sense of dread. Perhaps it was the fact that seeing those numbers in black and white brought the reality of our financial situation to life. That being said, the only thing that helped us to put the cork back into our hemorrhaging piggy bank was to take an honest, hard look at the money coming in and going out. Table 2 provides a sample breakdown of a typical household budget.

Table 2: Sample Household Budget

30%	Housing
18%	Transportation
16%	Food
8%	Miscellaneous
5%	Clothing
5%	Medical
5%	Recreation
5%	Utilities
4%	Savings
4%	Other Debts

www.practicalmoneyskills.com

The left hand column provides a suggested percentage of the monthly post-tax income that should be allotted for fixed and flexible costs. On the right-hand side, the costs are listed in descending order of percentage of overall budget.

This table is meant only as a guideline to help prepare a family budget. There is room for flexibility. If you live in an area of the country where mortgage costs are higher than the average, you will likely need to lower your percentage of flexible costs in order to have a successful monthly budget.

Calculate fixed costs

Determine your current fixed costs and calculate how they fit into the sample budget. Estimating fixed costs can only lead to trouble. Get out your bank statements for the last three months and determine the exact amount of money that you spend each month on:

✓ Mortgage or rent payments

✓ Car loan or lease payments

✓ Car insurance

✓ Gasoline (take a three month average)

✓ Groceries (take a three month average)

✓ Healthcare expenditures (include monthly premiums and medications purchased monthly)

✓ Credit cards (the amount that you owe will go down slightly each month, but if you pay the same amount instead of reducing the size of your payment, your debt will be reduced more quickly)

✓ Student loan payments

✓ Utilities (take a three month average)

✓ Other (include any bills that must be paid monthly not already on this list, including a reasonable clothing allowance).

Don't forget to plan ahead for some of the miscellaneous costs that you will incur during residency. The interview trail for residency or fellowship positions can present an unanticipated expense. Airline tickets and hotel costs are often not reimbursed when interviewing for training positions. Putting money into a savings account to cover some of these non-negotiable costs will help to absorb some of the costs that you will have. Fees for sitting the board exams during fellowship or immediately following residency can also be expensive. The boards alone can easily cost more than $1000. This does not include expenses for travel or accommodations including hotel, rental cars and eating out. Budgeting in advance for these expenses will reduce your financial stress as you move ahead through the training years.

Find room for flexible costs

After you've recovered from the shock of how much money has to go out the door each month, determine how much you have left over. Using your bank and credit card statements for the last three months, determine how much money you are spending above and beyond your fixed costs. Take an inventory of your flexible costs:

- ✓ Clothing (Prada bags and Manolo Blahnik alligator boots are unfortunately not necessities.)

- ✓ Dining Out (yes, the morning Starbucks counts too.)

- ✓ Recreation (movies, amusement parks, sporting events or trips to local museums)

- ✓ Gifts (baby showers, birthdays and holidays)

- ✓ Mad money (craft projects, books, and DVDs)

Putting the fixed and flexible costs together

You don't need to buy a fancy financial software package for the computer to calculate your budget and determine whether or not you are living within your means. The internet has taken financial health to an all new level, making it easier to put the pieces of your financial puzzle together. The list of financial planning websites gets longer every day, but the following two suggestions are what I consider *tried and true*:

Mint
www.mint.com
Join the online banking craze and get an overview of your financial expenditures by joining Mint. This free program allows you to pull together your finances, track spending and set savings goals and can even be accessed through a mobile phone application.

Budget Pulse
www.budgetpulse.com
The Budget Pulse program does not sync with any of your bank or financial institutions, but it does offer free tools to help you get an overview of where you stand financially and get out of debt or save for big ticket items.

At the end of the day though, if you are paying for groceries with credit cards, are dipping into your overdraft every month or have to take out a loan to shift your debt around, you don't need debt management software to know that your financial health may be in jeopardy. I know that the next statement will result in a lot of forehead slapping and proclamations of "well, duh", but I'm going to say this anyway. Your monthly fixed and flexible costs combined should not exceed your net monthly income.

I'm not trying to be offensive by stating the obvious. Why say it then? My husband and I have done too much of our share of magical financial planning through the years for me to not break it down like this (and maybe saying it out loud helps me to firm this up in my own mind). Though money management tools can be fun and even helpful, use common sense to remind yourself of your financial reality. Whatever the result of your initial budget and financial planning, being honest with yourself is the first step to taking charge of your money.

Ummmmmm

If you have gone through your bank and credit card statements and have discovered that you are paying for fixed costs like groceries with your credit cards, do not despair. You are not alone. Many medical spouses have been in the same position as they struggle to balance student loan payments with the rising cost of living. I personally know how awful it feels to realize that not only is the dream house out of reach, but so is the morning coffee at Starbucks. All is not lost, but it is important to rein it in before your finances spiral out of control. Counting on future income to eradicate consumer debt or repair credit damage created during training is unwise.

One thing that immediately stands out of the sample budget is *Other Debts*, which is tucked away at the bottom of the list. This includes things like student loan payments and consumer debt. It is certainly a number to keep in mind when considering taking out more student loan debt, physician loans or before you whip out that credit card. Though many residents are able to defer loan payments until after residency is over, when you are planning your post-training budget, if you go over 4%, you'll have to cut back in other areas. That means that you may not be able to buy the house that you want, finally purchase a second car or get rid of that garage sale furniture like you had planned. It's a good motivator to help keep debt as low as possible during medical training. Preparing a good budget now and sticking with it is hard, but it is the best way to avoid financial frustration later.

It might not be possible right now to climb out of debt until training is over, but stopping the painful financial downslide is a realistic goal. Consider transferring all of your higher interest credit card debt to one single lower interest card. Another option is to take out a physician loan to pay off your debt.

SunTrust bank offers a loan program for physicians in training. Medical students and residents can borrow money and then make interest only payments until up to two years post training. (This can be extended at times with special permission).

> **SunTrust**
> **www.suntrust.com**
> For more information about the features of a SunTrust physician loan, visit their personal finance portal. An application can be completed online or by telephone.

Loan amounts vary by training year and have a range of between $5000-$75.000. Table 3 provides information about the current loan limits based on the training year that you are in.

Table 3: 2011 SunTrust Loan Limits

PGY I	Up to $25,000
PGY II	Up to $30,000
PGY III	Up to $35,000
PGY IV and Fellows	Up to $40,000
Final Year of Training and Signed Contract	Up to $45,000
In Practice	Up to $75,000

www.suntrust.com/portal/server.pt/community/ rate_terms_conditions/559

There are a few important words of caution. Currently, the fixed interest rate for SunTrust is below 10%. Variable rates are a little lower, but that fluctuates depending on the prime rate. Obviously, if your credit card debt is at a lower interest rate, it makes no financial sense to borrow from SunTrust. Taking out large loan amounts to pay for other merchandise could become very expensive at that interest rate. Use this option only if it makes better financial sense than doing what you are doing now. Additionally, if you take out a loan to pay off credit card debt, it is crucial that you also either cancel your credit cards once you transfer balances or put them away and don't use them. It would be terrible to lighten the financial load by consolidating your debt only to end up spending again and getting further in the hole.

Visit with a financial planner

It is never too early to sit down and discuss your short and long-term financial goals with a professional who can help you to review your debt, investments and savings. There are services that cater to medical families. These companies have insight into how student loan debt and years of medical school and residency training can negatively impact your finances. They can help with retirement planning, portfolio-building and can offer general suggestions about home purchases and other big financial decisions like life insurance, long-term care insurance and estate planning. The idea of sitting down with a financial planner never occurred to us during training or in the first few years while we adjusted to life after fellowship. As a consequence, we made some mistakes that have come back to haunt us. Though we paid off debt, we never purchased life insurance or long term care insurance for me. I was young and it didn't occur to either of us that something might happen to make obtaining that insurance more difficult. My cancer diagnosis at 35 may have put an end to my ability to ever secure affordable life insurance. Not preparing better for the unexpected is something that my husband and I both regret.

There are several companies that work with physicians and their families. As you are researching them, you should not feel pressured to invest or to give out names of family members and friends. Interview potential advisors and don't hesitate to walk away if you feel uncomfortable. Some companies to consider include:

North Star Resource Group (www.northstarfinancialmd.com) A Minnesota based financial group that was established in 2003 that is active in most US states. They specialize in the management of personal and educational loan debt as well as helping their clients to achieve financial health.

Investor Solutions (www.investorsolutions.com/services/financial-planning-for-physicians)
This fee-only company from Florida offers flexible scheduling and help with wealth-building.

Whatever approach you decide on to get your finances under control, it's important to budget and plan today so that your family's future financial health is sound.

Chapter 16

Bigger, better, more.

Money talks-but credit has an echo.
—Bob Thaves

In the past 20 years, the cost of a medical education has increased 165% for private schools and 312% for public schools (American Medical Student Association). It is not uncommon now for graduates to leave medical school with between $100,000 and $250,000 in debt. With the cost of tuition continuing to rise and resident salaries remaining low in relationship to the debt, consumer debt incurred during residency and fellowship only serves to magnify the financial obligations of families as they move on from training. Avoid the "we will be able to pay it off later" trap. Educate yourself on loan repayment amounts early and then make informed choices about increasing your debt during residency and fellowship.

FinAid
www.finaid.org/calculators/scripts/
loanpayments.cgi
Estimate your monthly student loan payments and determine the amount of money that you will need to earn in order to comfortably afford to pay the loan amounts back. With Stafford loans currently at 6.8%, paying off $125,000 in loans over 30 years will cost just over $800/month. You will need to earn $100,000/year to pay this amount off. This does not include any consumer debt that you might have.

Once you have recovered from the shock of your monthly loan repayment amount, resolve to minimize further expenses as much as possible.

Stick with your budget

Creating a budget is the easy part. Following through and making changes in spending behavior is hard. Very hard. It is easy to give into temptation and buy the gourmet coffee or the shirt you found on sale when you are feeling the pinch of too much Q3 call.

"We work hard. We deserve to buy something fun," has been uttered so many times around this house that we believe it to be true. What we sometimes forget is that the reward for hard work can be spending time together or enjoying what we already have. Veering from the family budget can result in much more stress later, even if it is fun to buy new gadgets or eat out frequently.

If you find yourself slowly drifting away from your carefully crafted budget, put on the brakes before any real damage is done. The first indication that I am veering off of the beaten path is that I start frequenting drive-thrus for a coffee or diet coke. I rationalize my decision by telling myself that it is *only* a dollar. One dollar quickly becomes five dollars if I buy myself a drink each day. Diet coke is my gateway drug. Once I start spending on little stuff, I tend to lose control. I move on to Starbucks and then my budget really gets blown.

No one is perfect and backslides happen. Once you realize that you are slipping back into your old ways, revisit your budget and give yourself a pep talk. For an extra kick in the pants, estimate the money you have spent in a single week on unnecessary extras. That should scare you straight again.

Plan before you shop

Before you head out the door for the grocery store, *Target* or *Gymboree*, make a list of the things that you need to buy. This sounds like such a simple suggestion and yet it can be hard to follow through with. If you plan your meals in advance and take an inventory of your refrigerator and cupboards you will be less likely to purchase things that you don't need. Back-to-school shopping? Go through the kids' drawers and decide in advance what clothes you need to buy. Write those lists and then stick with them.

Wal-Mart used to be our worst problem. We would go in to get diapers and would come out with shoes for the kids, new pots, a tablecloth, a DVD and a variety of items that we never even used. There was a time that we weren't able to leave without spending at least $100. After we came down from our post-shopping rush, we would promise each other that *next time* we wouldn't spend as much. Our *aha* moment changed all that. We no longer browse when we go shopping. If we need shoes for the kids, that is what we get.

If you have plastic, you can eat

For months, the sign at our local *Subway* read, "If you have plastic, you can eat". Every time I drove by and read it, I cringed, because

I know how difficult it can be to resist the temptation when you are short on cash and are feeling entitled to a treat. Heed this advice: Leave the credit cards at home. Nothing gets in the way of a sound financial plan more than seeing something that you feel like you just can't live without and knowing that you have plastic in your pocket that would only require you to make a small monthly payment to buy it. Forget that with interest you would be paying for the item three times over. Eventually, your spouse's income will go up and you can pay it off then, right? If you see yourself in this in any way, go collect all of your credit cards, throw them in a pot of water and stick the pot in the freezer. If anything, you will be required to come home and think about your purchase while the ice is melting. If it is important enough you can buy it the next day.

Pay cash for your purchases and you will save money. It's just too easy to throw unintended extras into the shopping cart when you are paying with your debit or credit card. If you know that you only have cash in your pockets you will limit your spending. For some reason, cash is also just harder to spend.

If our finances start getting out of hand, I still go back to paying cash each week for my groceries. To keep my costs low, I also throw in the added incentive that any money left over is mad money for me to spend on myself or on a treat for the kids. This motivates me to stick to my grocery lists and only buy what is necessary. As a result, I can save enough money for a frivolous purchase over time.

Put it on layaway

Layaway is a simple way to buy an item, pay over a period of time and avoid interest charges. I am a big fan of avoiding any additional finance charges. Despite the fact that we have been out of training for years and we have more disposable income than we did during residency, I still regularly put things on layaway. Layaway can allow you to pay for an item that you just can't resist over a period of a couple of months. It can also give you an inexpensive *out* if you decide in the end that you don't want the item after all (usually, you just lose the initial layaway fee).

I really got into quilting one year and was determined to make a quilt for each of my family members. Our local craft store had just received a new shipment of quilt kits. I was so excited that I snatched up several kits. I purchased one on the spot to get started and put the others on layaway. It was a good thing, too. I never did finish that first kit and I was able to cancel my layaway.

Buy it second hand

Second hand resale or consignment shops that boast gently used items can be a great way to save money on must-have items. Our local *Once Upon A Child* sells used cribs, bedding, toddler beds, strollers, play sets, toys and clothing all for a fraction of the price that we would spend buying these things new. To find a local *Once Upon A Child* store, visit their store locator at **www.ouac. com**.

The best part, of course, about second hand shops is that it is possible to bring in your own items for sale. Hold onto baby clothes, toys (and the original boxes that they come in for a little extra money), and other household items. If they are in good shape, you may be able to earn back a little money on your original investment in them. Many second hand shops offer money on the spot for items in good condition. Most consignment stores price your item and then give you a percentage of the proceeds after the items have sold.

Consider shopping at Goodwill or a similar thrift shop for household items. It is possible to find good quality furniture, tableware, clothing, and holiday decorations at very reasonable prices. Be cautious when purchasing furniture second hand. Make sure that the items don't smell of cigarette smoke. Though there is a copious amount of advice online to get rid of the odor, I can testify that none of them really work.

> **Goodwill Locator**
> **http://locator.goodwill.org**
> Use the Goodwill locator to find the
> Goodwill stores in your area.

Of course, no discussion of buying things second hand can conclude without mentioning *Craigslist* and *eBay*. A local search of *Craigslist* can help you find anything from Victorian sofas to toilets. *Ebay* proudly boasts "Whatever it is, you can get it here" and for the most part, that's true. That being said, it can be hard to hunt down a real bargain there.

> **eBay**
> **www.ebay.com**
> If you are looking for something specific,
> chances are you can find it on *eBay*. Bid for
> items in an auction format and then complete
> your transaction online.
>
> **Craigslist**
> **www.craigslist.org**
> Consider yourself warned. This website is
> addictive. You can find anything you need and
> many things that you don't by searching the
> pages of *Craigslist*. The transactions usually
> take place via email and are more personal.

My first Craigslist purchase was a 1970's pop-up trailer. I bought it for $300 and then put in at least another $700 renovating it over time. I had to tear out the roof, put in new floors and refinish all of the wood surfaces. I thought it was a great deal, and I learned a lot of new skills. My husband was slightly less impressed though. The initial $300 hadn't fit into our budget at the time. The extra money to renovate it was an even bigger bite out of our budget. I can get so excited by the good deals that I sometimes lose sight of our goals.

Shop the sales

A good friend of mine and I have a fun holiday tradition competition. We search the after Christmas sales and try to find the least expensive gift to give each other the next year. The goal is to find something truly gift-worthy but to spend only a few dollars. The person who finds the best gift for the least amount of money is the winner. I can truly say that few things give me more satisfaction than finding $55 sweaters for $5.00, plush holiday blankets for $2.00 or picking up all of my stocking stuffers for the kids for next to nothing. I often can accomplish most of my Christmas shopping for the year before summer comes.

I like to buy the gift bags, tissue paper and wrapping paper when the holidays are over and save them for the next year too. I have a tendency to buy generic gifts like holiday picture frames, candles and holiday jewelry when they come into the 80% clearance days. I pack them in individual gift bags in January, line them up on a shelf in my closet and rest easy knowing that I will have gifts ready to go for a surprise visit from a friend or a holiday party the next year.

Many stores send out weekly circulars detailing their sales, and good deals can be found at the ends of the aisles or in clearance sections of department or toy stores at odd times during the year. It might feel a little bit odd to buy the Halloween decorations in January or to pick up Christmas plates in March, but it beats paying full price when the appropriate season finally rolls around. This is a good way to stock up on children's birthday party gifts and items for your own family throughout the year too.

Compare before you buy

If you have your heart set on a certain item, don't run out to the nearest shop and buy it . . . just yet. There are a variety of virtual sources that will provide you with product reviews and help you to find the best local or online price.

Fat Wallet
www.fatwallet.com
Find coupons and promo codes, discount prices and special price deals on products from leading retailers. This is a website that belongs in your bookmarks.

PriceGrabber
www.pricegrabber.com
PriceGrabber is another online resource that allows you to look for the lowest price on products. In addition, you can read reviews written about the merchants selling the products.

MySimon
www.mysimon.com
My Simon offers a unique *compare* feature. Search for a product and then view all of the stores where it is available while you compare the price differences.

Finally, be sure and check out **Amazon.com** before you buy anything. Many new and used items are available through their Marketplace at a fraction of the cost of other stores. We purchased the entire *Series of Unfortunate Events* for less than $.25/book for our oldest child when he was reading them one summer.

Clip coupons

I'm not a big coupon clipper. It isn't that I don't appreciate the savings that I can reel in. The truth is that I'm just lazy. I've had some inspired moments (particularly after watching an episode of *extreme couponing*) but my enthusiasm tends to wear off as I try to sort through my coupon bounty and the items on sale at our grocery store. I imagine getting all of my grocery items for free, and quickly realize that I don't have the time or energy to come close to that. I sometimes lose sight of the fact that saving something is better than not saving at all. There are several websites that cater to those of us who know what we want and don't want to spend a lot of time hunting down coupons.

Groupon
www.groupon.com
Groupon is a website that offers deep discounts on on a variety of products from top retailers. You have to purchase the discount coupons at the Groupon website, but then they are honored by the retailers. It is possible to save 60% or more on select items including restaurant meals, furniture, bath items and more. Membership is free. It is definitely worth looking at.

Ebates
www.ebates.com
Forget clipping coupons altogether. Ebates offers cash back on purchases through their website to over 1200 top retailers. Saving money is free and is as easy as signing up with your email address. Your account is credited with 1-4% cash back on purchases up to four times a year.

Resist temptation

Once I get my heart set on a certain item, it takes a relentless hold of my thoughts. Most recently, I began shopping the post-holiday sales for Christmas decorations. Forget the fact that the motorized reindeer that I bought at last year's sale never made it out of its box this season. I continued to find items that I felt I absolutely needed to buy for the next year. The decorations that caught my eye were the large, plastic ornament balls for hanging on outside trees. At 75% off, I considered them a steal and bought a few for our pine tree in the front yard. Then the thought occurred to me that I could decorate all of the trees in our backyard with these colorful, unbreakable ornaments. As I mentally calculated the number of balls I needed to buy, it became clear to me that I needed to stay away from the stores completely. There will always be good deals to lure me in. For the record, we had a winter storm that blew away the balls that I had purchased. They were never recovered.

When temptation strikes, sometimes the best avenue is simply avoidance. If you find yourself coming home with *great deals* on a frequent basis, it might be time to stop heading out to the shopping mall altogether until you regain control.

One of the many challenges of medical training is finding a way to minimize the additional debt that you acquire beyond money owed for student loans. The expenses for moving, interviewing and simply surviving month-to-month can overwhelm a family's budget. It's also understandable to feel like you are working hard and deserve to treat yourself. You should pamper yourself from time-to-time, but consider your budget and your future financial goals carefully before giving in to the urge.

Chapter 17

Want what you have

Do what you can, with what you have, where you are.
—Theodore Roosevelt

Does a trip to the mall leave you drooling over the latest fashions? Anytime I watch re-runs of HGTV's *I Want That*, I decide that I can't live without the newest trend. Who doesn't want to enjoy the newest craze in educational baby toys, purses, shoes or interior design? It feels good to pamper ourselves with the most modern technical gadgets and household amenities. Well, it feels good until the bill comes. There are other ways to indulge without breaking the bank. Ultimately, it all comes down to working with what you already own.

Clean house emotionally

Before you head out to the mall to buy a new outfit or submit your shopping cart at your favorite website, ask yourself one question:

Do I really need this?

For me, most of the time, the answer that echoes through my mind is a resounding "No". My husband is the worst emotional shopper that I have ever met though. If the doorbell rings and it is the postman asking me to sign for another German book or movie delivery, I know that he is feeling overwhelmed or upset about something.

It's not uncommon to turn to shopping therapy when we feel like something is missing in our lives. You work hard and you deserve to pamper yourself. The problem is that often times buying things is a way to try and fill a void in our lives. It is okay to treat ourselves from time-to-time as a reward, but take your emotional temperature before you go shopping. Are you about to whip out the credit card for something to make you feel better because your spouse has Q3 call and you are feeling lonely, or do you really need a new pair of shoes for work?

Want what you already have in your life, and then decide whether or not you are shopping out of necessity or a need to soothe your feelings.

Reorganize, Rearrange, Refresh

Is the garage sale furniture that you bought for your first apartment back when you started college an eyesore in your living room now? When you are on a tight training budget, it seems like one of the lowest financial priorities is decorating your home. After paying the rent, utilities and groceries, extras like a new dining room table or sofa with loveseat are often just not realistic. Before you start engaging in furniture stores drive-bys to see what is new in home design, decide how you can get the look that you want with the items that you already own. Making a few simple changes in your room can give you the feeling of new for only a fraction of the cost.

Paint

Pick out a few color samples from your local home improvement shop. Bring them home, try them out and then get to work painting a room or simply creating a focal wall. Changing the color of your walls can give your home a more elegant, personalized look without breaking the bank. The good news is that if you outgrow the colors, you can repaint again later. I say good news. My husband says "someone please stop her". The last time I attempted to paint, I backed into a freshly painted wall and ended up with beige paint all over my . . . . gluteus maximus. I immediately removed my pants to soak them in soap and water and walked back into the living room sans pants. At about this time, my first-grader let a neighbor in to talk to me. Imagine the collective feelings of surprise that filled the room as I stood there without pants on. It's all good. With a lot of therapy, I think I will get past it.

Rearrange

Take an inventory of the furniture that you own. Can you repurpose what you own to save you money while you work towards finishing training? Is the arm chair in the guest bedroom begging to be moved into the living room? We had a big, soft, blue chair (that I had found at a used furniture store) wasting away in our downstairs guest bedroom for several years. I don't remember how it found its way downstairs, but it might have been during one of my earlier attempts at rearranging furniture. As my husband's home office slowly started to take shape, we began looking for an affordable, comfortable chair to put by the window for him to sit in while he read. We looked at several furniture stores but just weren't at a point where investing in a chair made financial sense for us. The forgotten chair found a new home in his office

With an accent pillow, it looked like a new piece of furniture. We were pleasantly surprised to discover that by rearranging what we had, we could get the look we were going for.

Move around your existing furniture to create a more open, inviting space in your house or to change the look of a room. Making a small investment in a new slipcover for your sofa or some accent pillows can net a big emotional payoff, because even a small change can have a noticeable impact. Arrange your living room around a focal point or move your bed to the other side of your bedroom. Changing the layout of your room can give the space a brand new feel.

Declutter

Clutter is my greatest enemy. With five children, I always have someone's school papers, pens, books, colored pencils and candy wrappers littering my counter tops, sofas and at times (like most of the time) even the floor. Each of our children has a cubby to keep their coats and school bags in and yet I still trip over their books and shoes when I'm walking down the hall.

Eliminating clutter and organizing your collectibles, book shelves, desktops and other visible spaces can help you to achieve a more comfortable home. To reduce clutter, put a basket in each main room of your house. When you clean up, toss anything that doesn't belong in that room into the basket. Once you have moved from room to room and have established some order, go back to your clutter baskets. At the end of the day, spend a half an hour returning the items to their rightful place in your home (or trip over the baskets from one week to the next, which approaches my method).

Clean and Repair

My mother-in-law visits us twice a year from Germany. Her suitcase is usually packed full of toys and books for the kids, chocolates for my husband, and cleaning rags for me. *Special* cleaning rags. In the weeks leading up to her arrival, I busy myself cleaning all of the areas that she pointed out to me a half of a year earlier. I swear she thinks that if she didn't come, we might ultimately end up living in squalor. She is always checking things like the rubber seals on the dishwasher door to make sure I have kept up with the cleaning on them. Our toaster gets dumped over the sink to ensure that I have left no crumb unturned (Confession: I have resorted to buying a new toaster for these visits). As annoying as it is, my mother-in-law has owned the same toaster for well over 20 years and it still looks and functions like new. She takes immaculate care of her belongings and if something breaks, she has it repaired instead of buying new. She has had a new cord put on her iron. If she finds a sock with a hole in it, she repairs it instead of tossing it in the garbage. I hate to admit it, because I'm already hanging my head in shame a little here, but she is an incredible example of how to raise a family on a shoestring budget. Because of her sound financial management, she has been able to afford a much better retirement for herself, and her belongings are all in good shape. I respect her. I just can't say that out loud.

The stainless steel double oven is probably out of your price range right now, but you can get the look of new by simply washing and cleaning your appliances. Pull out the rubber gloves and tackle the grime in your microwave, oven or dishwasher. Your items will be clean, look nice and they will last longer. Refresh curtains, upholstery and carpeting by vacuuming them or having them cleaned. You can get the look of new again by simply giving what you own a deep cleaning.

Along those lines, taking some time to repair your furniture or appliances can save you money and help you to afford the bigger purchases when it is time to update. Following my mother-in-law's example, I have taken our vacuum cleaner in to have the cord replaced or the motor repaired on several occasions. Inconvenience aside, all of the repairs together have not added up to the cost of a new vacuum cleaner yet and it has remained serviced and in good working condition.

Spice up your wardrobe

Right. This is the part where I will try not to confess that I wear socks with my sandals, or that I have been known to show up at my kids' schools in Capri pants in the middle of a Minnesota winter. I am many things, but a fashion guru is not one of them. I cannot tell you when to stop wearing white or whether you are supposed to match your shoes to your bag. This is one of the many *do as I say, not as I do* moments.

The newest fashion trends may be out of your price range (and off of my radar completely), but you don't have to go into debt or engage in a major shopping spree to get a new look. If the clothes in your closet just aren't feeling fresh anymore, spend an afternoon sorting out your closets and drawers to take an inventory of what you already own.

Remix

Try mixing and matching new outfits from the clothes that you already own. My assumption here is that this is good advice for people who do have the knack for fashion and for people like me, who watch *What Not to Wear* and don't quite get the new rules. It's always fun to wear something a new way or pair a top with a different pair of slacks. At the end of the day, it is also cheaper than buying a new outfit.

Accessorize

Give an outfit a chic new look by adding inexpensive accessories like scarves, shoes, a new purse or matching costume jewelry. This is another way to celebrate a new look without spending a lot of money. There are outlet shops that cater to the bargain hunter on a mission to spend less and get more.

> **Sam Moon**
> **www.sammoon.com**
> Sam moon is a specialty store that sells costume jewelry, purses, accessories and other gift items at a discounted price. Visit their Dallas location or shop online for good deals for less.

Rent the Runway

Say what? Seriously, just when I thought that Netflix was the best thing since sliced bread, I discovered that it is not just possible to rent DVD's and have them delivered in the mail. It is possible to rent designer clothing, accessories and handbags to use for special occasions and then return them in the mail for no additional charge. I know. My head is spinning too.

> **Rent the Runway**
> **www.renttherunway.com**
> My gut says that if you can afford the cost of renting one of the fabulous runway dresses at Rent the Runway that you are in better financial shape than you think. That being said, if fashion is very important to you, this might be the most reasonable way for you to afford those designer duds for graduation from residency or a special party.
>
> **Bag Borrow or Steal**
> **www.bagborroworsteal.com**
> Rent by the week, month, or season and get great deals on designer handbags, jewelry, watches and more. Return the items in good condition and then look for more.

There are a variety of new rental websites that have set up shop online over the last few years. Finding that dress, bag or accessory might be easier than you thought.

Don't try and fill up your emotional reserves through shopping therapy. Find creative ways to use items that you already own, or invest in inexpensive accents to give your home or wardrobe a new look. Getting into more debt during training will only hurt your financial health later when you are looking at settling down into your post-training life. Someday, new appliances and trendy fashions will be in your budget.

Part Five
Relocation

Where we love is home-
home that our feet may leave, but not our hearts.
—Oliver Wendell Holmes Sr.

Moving.

The word alone sends my brain into shutdown mode. It immediately conjures up images in my mind of going through closets, cleaning out the garage, runs to *Good Will* to drop off clothing and old toys, cleaning, packing, and arguing.

Without a doubt, one of the most stressful and challenging aspects of the medical training journey centers around the inevitable moves necessary for medical school, residency, and fellowship. The prospects of packing the house, moving across the country and starting over can be intimidating at best. There are few things as unsettling as realizing that in a matter of months or even weeks you will be living in a new town and will be facing unknown challenges. Perhaps the most positive way to look at the moves is to recognize them as being a part of the adventure of medical training. This of course is easier said than done when you are in the throes of packing or miss having family and friends nearby.

When my husband first began his residency training, we were living in Stuttgart, Germany. Early on, he decided that he was interested in pursuing an Infectious Disease fellowship. This specialty training is not offered in Germany and so we began the long process of relocating to the United States. To help him with his English skills, we decided to do a year of training in the United Kingdom. My husband arranged interviews throughout the United Kingdom, including Northern Ireland. We flew out to London with our six month old son only a few days later. We rented a car at Heathrow airport and I navigated the winding roads while he prepared for his interviews. This basically consisted of me driving, reading the map and settling the baby while he slept in the passenger seat. In retrospect, I realize that this was truly a foreshadowing of things to come.

The most exciting part of our journey began the evening before we were to take the Ferry from Stranrear, Scotland over to Northern Ireland. We had booked a hotel room in Northern England only to discover that the roads were more torturous than we had imagined. Instead of the fast, Autobahn-style highway traveling that we were used to, we were forced onto single lane roads that wound through one small town after the next. As much as I enjoyed the site-seeing expedition, it quickly became clear to us both that we would not make it to Stranrear by morning unless we drove through the night.

We stopped for dinner and planned our course before heading out into the early evening. I remember little about that night other than being gripped by fear as I drove along a perilously small, winding road with no visible light other than my headlights or those of passing cars. The road snaked through what appeared to be a heavily wooded area, but it was actually so dark that I couldn't tell for sure. Unlike the bright lights lining American streets, the Scottish landscape loomed like shadows in a dimly lit cave. As my husband and son soundly slept through the night, I found myself wedged between two large trucks. Our rental car rocked back and forth as I clung to the left side of the road. I uttered more than one prayer, and admittedly more than one obscenity as the night went on.

We arrived in Stranrear with two hours to spare before the ferry left for Northern Ireland. I parked the car near the docks and drifted in and out of sleep before the rising sun stirred us awake. We were finally allowed to board the ferry.

Within a few short hours, we were driving again . . . this time towards Craigavon Area Hospital near Portadown, Northern Ireland. The residency position turned out to be a great opportunity for my husband. When he was offered a contract, he signed it the same day. Our adventure had officially begun.

Chapter 18

There's no place like home

Life is like a game of cards. The hand that is dealt you represents determinism; the way you play it is free will.
—**Jawaharlal Nehru**

Whether you have your spouse's medical school admission letter in your hand or are nervously checking online to see if the *Match* results are posted, the wait is finally over. You may be disappointed to discover that you will be moving far away from family (or may be overjoyed), but now that the uncertainty is a thing of the past, you can embrace the task of finding a new place to live.

One of the first decisions that you and your spouse will have to make is whether or not you are going to purchase a home or rent. There is still some debate about whether or not it is financially wise to purchase a home during medical school or residency training. This is a personal decision that depends a lot on your own finances, the length of time that you will be living in the home and the geographic location of your training program.

Show me the money

Buying a home is exciting and can even be a good financial investment. It probably goes without saying, but it is also expensive. Before you get online and start looking at homes, consider the following expenses that you will have to pay upfront.

Home Inspection fee: This can run anywhere from $175 to $325 or more depending on the size and age of your home as well as its location.

Down Payment: Most banks require you to make a minimum down payment of 2-5 percent. On a home that costs 100,000 that would mean paying a minimum of $2000-$5000 upfront. Some lenders do have home loan programs that do not require a down payment. If you are certain that you want to purchase a home and are interested in a loan with 0% down, contact local banks to inquire about their mortgage programs.

Before you apply for a loan, check your credit report to make sure that there are no blemishes on your record (well, at least none that you weren't aware of). The major credit reporting agencies are a good place to visit for that information.

TransUnion
www.transunion.com
TransUnion is one of the national registries
that posts credit information.

Equifax
www.equifax.com
Equifax offers a variety of products for
consumers to check their credit report, FICO
score or monitor their credit report for
fraud.

Experian
www.experian.com
With the Experian website it is possible to
check your credit reports with all three credit
reporting agencies (Experian, Transunion
and Equifax) at one time.

Researching your credit score in advance of a loan application is important. If there are any discrepancies you will have time to petition to have them removed. I hate that I have a personal anecdote about this. When we moved for fellowship, we ultimately had to choose an apartment community in a matter of about three hours. Though the Office of Medical Education had shared a list of rental communities which catered to residents and fellows with us, the large size of our family meant that we had to find something less expensive. We ended up in an apartment community next to a well-known drug and prostitute complex. Of course we didn't know this until our moving van pulled in and the driver asked us point blank why we were moving there. There were needles on the playground and the area made me feel uncomfortable.

At the end of our one year lease, we moved to a rental home. Our walk-through was unremarkable, and we were promised our deposit back. Once we moved out, we were charged for damages to the apartment that we had not caused. Without our knowledge a report was made to our credit reporting agency. This was all sorted out after we hired an attorney who discovered fraudulent activity taking place in the office of the apartment complex. It was nerve-shattering and took the entire last year of fellowship to clear up.

I will just assume that you have no blemishes on your record and that you won't be moving into an apartment complex next to prostitutes and move on.

There are several financial institutions that cater to the needs of physicians and their families. These lenders offer a variety of home loan programs to medical families. You may still get a better deal at a local bank or credit union, but it is certainly worth your while to investigate all options:

Physician Loans
www.physicianloans.com
Physician Loans also has offered a unique *Doctor Loan* mortgage with 100% financing and no PMI since 1993. These loan packages are available for medical students and residents as well as attending physicians.

NADA
www.nadonline.com
The National Association of Doctors provides loans with zero money down and no PMI to residents as well as attending physicians.

EPL
www.exclusivephysicianloans.com
Exclusive Physician Loans is an organization dedicated to helping physicians secure home loans. They offer financing that is tailored to the unique needs of physicians.

Physician Relocation Specialists
www.physicianrelo.com
The Physician Relocation Specialists are connected with realtors and mortgage brokers that provide services specifically designed to meet the needs of busy medical families. They can help you to find a realtor and secure the best loan package possible.

SunTrust
https://www.suntrust.com/PersonalBanking/Loans/
PhysicianLoans
SunTrust does not only offer unsecured lines of credit to medical students, residents, and attending physicians. They are also able to offer mortgage packages to physicians. Visit their website for contact information.

In addition to the initial money that you will need to pay upfront, consider the extra costs involved in home ownership. Are you in the financial position to be able to pay for the upkeep on your new investment? This would include things like painting the walls and making updates to keep the home ready to sell when you move on for residency, fellowship or that attending job. Can you afford home repairs like a broken line to your septic tank?

During fellowship, we eventually settled into a rental house. One morning when my husband was taking a shower, he noticed that water was bubbling back up through the drain. He turned off the water and called me in to look at it with him. We huddled around the shower watching water from our sewer system hiccup up through the drain. The repair to the septic tank took several days. Because there was a crack in our pipes and sewage in our backyard we were forced to stay in a hotel until the tank was pumped and the crack was repaired. If we had been homeowners, we would have had had to pay for this little misadventure. It would have cost us several thousand dollars. Fortunately, because we were renters, the home owner paid our repairs and our hotel stay.

Of course, Murphy's Law seemed to dictate our entire fellowship experience and you may sail through home ownership without roof repairs, septic tank leaks or other costly surprises.

Finally, consider issues like general home maintenance. Who is going to mow your lawn, trim back the bushes, or shovel the driveway? Keep in mind that a *post*-call resident is unlikely to embrace these tasks on a regular basis. You'll be lucky to get your spouse to pick up his white coat after he tosses it onto the floor on his way to bed. Unless he buys a programmable robotic mowing machine you will either have to declare your grass an endangered species or mow the lawn yourself. As a result of the resident's busy schedule, many home maintenance chores will be added to your own growing list of things to do unless you are able to hire someone to do them for you. For the male medical spouse, the issue of mowing the lawn and general home maintenance may not be such a large issue, but added on top of the laundry, cooking and cleaning, it may just be a relief to minimize the workload during training.

Doing hard time

The length of time that you have been sentenced to the residency program is another important factor to take into consideration. The first few years of home ownership involve paying down more on the interest than the principal of your loan. Acquiring equity comes later. In addition, you have also invested money in a down payment and you may have to invest additional money in the upkeep of your home.

When you are ready to sell the home, you may also lose up to 7.5% to your realtor.

Investigate the current interest rates on homes, home prices in the area you are moving to, the amount of your down payment and how long you are planning to live in your home. You may discover that it is still worth the investment to buy a home for that three year internal medicine residency program or five year surgical residency sentence. Alternatively, you may decide that you wouldn't make a good return on your investment and would be better off renting. Of course, if you are like us, the bank might just laugh at your application and the decision will be made for you.

Go right to the horse's mouth

Don't guess about whether or not the medical students or residents who have gone before you have had trouble selling their homes and whatever you do, don't take the realtor's word for it. Before making a decision about renting or buying, talk with other medical students or residents if possible to find out whether or not those who do buy their homes have any difficulty selling them when they move on. This is certainly an important factor to consider in smaller communities and may be a big consideration for you if you are concerned about having to sell your home at the end of training while preparing to relocate.

We did not purchase a home during residency. I will be the first to admit that I was very disappointed about this. During moments of indulgent self-pity (and yes, I had many of those times) I felt like we were at a point in our lives where we were supposed to own a home. I compared our lifestyle to our friends who had chosen different professional paths. Our friends who had become teachers, nurses, and computer programmers all owned nice starter homes with fenced in backyards for their children to play in. They weren't spending much more than we were on their house payments. I felt like we had been *had*. I often drove by houses that were for sale and dreamed of the time that we would finally be able to own our own home.

My self-serving pity parties came to an end when I realized that several of the residents were having trouble selling their homes as training drew to a close. Though most of them did eventually sell their houses and townhomes, it was not without significant stress. As we wound down from training and prepared to move, I was so overwhelmed as it was just packing the house and preparing the children, that I thanked the banking gods that had denied us our home. I was relieved that I didn't have to clean the house to show it while packing the toys, playing *Chutes and Ladders* and finding a moving company. I didn't have to worry that we couldn't buy a new home until we sold the old one. We could just pack the house and leave without looking back. Of course, for every resident who had trouble selling their home, there was one who was able to sell their house within hours of putting it on the market. If you feel financially ready and are willing to take the risk then the emotional side of me that really wanted that Cape Cod with the white picket fence still says *go for it*.

Getting started

Once you have made a decision about whether or not you would like to rent or buy, you can begin to put together the pieces of this relocation jigsaw puzzle. The first thing you will want to consider is how close you would like to live to the hospital. A long commute for a *post*-call resident is probably not ideal. At the same time, if you have school-aged children, it may also be more important to consider the school district you will be living in.

A good place to begin your search is the medical school or residency program *Office of Medical Education*. Several schools and residency programs maintain basic information about local apartment complexes where medical families live. They may also provide you with more detailed information about areas of town that are safe to live in or provide you with names and numbers of students or residents willing to help out newcomers. Some residency programs also provide inexpensive on-campus housing options for their residents. Arm yourselves with questions before you call. These could include:

- ✓ Do you offer on-campus housing for medical students/ residents? If so, be sure and get the number of the housing office to find out about the cost as well as how to get on the waiting list.

- ✓ What part of town do most medical students/residents live? What are good school districts in the area?

- ✓ Are there any students or residents that we could contact to find out more information about housing?

- ✓ Does the medical school/residency program have a medical spouse alliance program that we can contact for more information?

- ✓ Are there any inexpensive hotels near the University/ Hospital campus that we can stay when we come house hunting.

Don't be shy about asking questions. Some of the most helpful suggestions that we got along the way, came from friendly secretaries who were more than happy to help. The web is another good place to find information:

Homefair
www.homefair.com
Homefair is a comprehensive website that provides a variety of articles to help you plan your move. It allows you to calculate the cost of your move, compare salaries and the costs of living in different cities and states, and view detailed reports from local schools.

Sperling's Best Places
www.bestplaces.net
Benefit from Bert Sperling's sixteen years of analyzing data from cities throughout the United States. Best Places offers information about the cost of living, real estate market, crime rates and local climate. In addition, members can sign on to provide a review of their city.

Real estate agents can also be another valuable resource. They are able to help you find rental homes, identify good school districts and provide you with information about the area in addition to their traditional role of selling homes. To get an idea of home prices in the area and to find out what homes are available, there are several good websites to help you get started:

Realtor.com
www.realtor.com
Realtor.com is a good place to begin searching for available homes. Be advised that the listings are not always up-to-date so if you do find your dream home, be sure and contact your local realtor.

Rent.com
www.rent.com
The Rent.com website is another resource that allows you to search through available rental homes and apartments. To view details of any search results you do need to fill out a short registration form and provide an email address.

Begin searching for your home or apartment as soon as you have found out where you will be moving. The *Match* results usually are available in mid-March, which gives you a little over three months to visit and find a suitable home, secure financing and plan a closing if necessary. Many homes come out onto the market in early spring. Be prepared to plan a short trip to meet with a realtor or visit an apartment complex before signing a contract. Moving in sight unseen can lead to difficult times if there are problems with your new living space.

As a final note, if you have decided to buy a house, avoid spending the maximum value that the bank is willing to approve you for unless you are certain that the payments will be manageable with your net income. Be sure to figure in any student loan payments and other fixed costs that might cut into your budget. As tempting as it is to get a few extra hundred square feet or the upgraded countertops, being house poor can ruin the fun of home ownership. Be realistic about what you can afford during residency. The white picket fence might not fit into the financial plan at this time, but one day it will. For now, it is important to recognize what is financially sensible. Act with your future financial interests in mind.

Chapter 19

Selling your home

It is a great piece of skill to know how to guide your luck,
even while waiting for it.
—Baltasar Gracian

Selling a home can be a daunting task. I have vivid childhood memories of racing through the house to do the ten minute tidy with my mom. Once the house was clean, we would throw all of our dirty laundry into the trunk of the car and drive off with it before a showing. My husband and I were pretty lucky with the sale of our first home. Murphy and his laws must have been on vacation because after a wild week of cleaning, repainting and repairs, we were able to sell the house quickly and avoid the unpleasant necessity of preparing for repeated showings.

If you are in the position of having to put your own home on the market during the end of medical school or residency, it may be comforting to know that many families have successfully sold their homes and moved on to the next stage of training, and you can too. Whether you will be using a realtor or are thinking about acting as your own agent, putting your house on the market is an undertaking that will require attention to detail and some good old-fashioned elbow grease.

Get your house shipshape

Before you put your house up for sale, you will need to dig in for the dirty job of getting it ready for the market. The idea of spending evenings and weekends cleaning and packing may not sound appealing, but it will pay off in the long run when you are able to sell your home more quickly for the price that you are asking.

Declutter

Start the packing process early by sorting through your belongings at least a month before you house goes on the market. Pack away items that you want to take with you, throw out what is no longer usable and give away or sell everything else. Rent a storage unit as you get closer to putting your house on the market and store all boxes and any extra furniture pieces that might be taking up usable space in your home. Strip your house down to the bare bones. It should be livable and comfortable, but free of as many knickknacks, books and decorations as possible.

Clean

This is my least favorite thing to do, but some people find this the most rewarding part of peeling back the layers of their home. Before the realtor comes in to price your house or the *For Sale* sign is posted in the yard, it is important to scrub, scour, wipe, clean and polish. It seem obvious that the gunk that has been living on the seatbelt of the highchair for the last three months needs to cleaned up, but beyond the everyday cleaning tasks are things like washing down:

- ✓ Walls

- ✓ Baseboards

- ✓ Windows

- ✓ Window sills

- ✓ Doors and door frames

- ✓ Blinds

In addition, don't forget to clean out:

- ✓ Light fixtures (vacuum them out and wash them if necessary)

- ✓ Shower doors and bathroom tiles

- ✓ Kitchen and bathroom drawers and cabinets

Please note that for some people that list does include their regular cleaning tasks. *C'est la vie.* When the entire house is clean, wash any dirty curtains, dust all shelves and woodwork and have your carpets steam cleaned. If you are feeling energetic, most grocery stores rent carpet cleaners for a minimal charge. It is well worth the investment to do it yourself if you feel like you can.

Repair

At some stage in the cleaning process, it's a good idea to make a list of any repairs that need to be made. When we moved from our last home, we had to replace a cabinet, repair a faucet and have an electrical outlet fixed. These were all things that had been on our to-do list for a while, but selling our home meant finally taking care of those pesky problems. If you have any issues that might affect the sale of your home, take care of them before your house is on the market. It might even be worth the investment to have your home inspected by a professional home inspector to guarantee that there are no major problems that need to be addressed. Nothing is worse for a home owner than losing a sale because of repairs that need to be made.

Organize

I will admit that because I am an instant-gratification kind of a girl, getting things organized in the house is something that I enjoy. Though I would never confess to this openly, I have to give my mother-in-law another nod for my clean cupboards and organized pantry. In the early years of my marriage, I took offense at the endless hours that she and I spent tidying, arranging and organizing. As the years passed, I realized that helping me to create a system out of the chaos that we sometimes live in is her way of showing me that she loves me. I have even learned to embrace her visits and appreciate her support.

There are a few areas of your home that prospective buyers may be looking at that are unanticipated (and possibly unwelcomed). Make sure that your kitchen and bathroom cupboards and drawers are clean, free of clutter and are organized. This is as simple as investing in some inexpensive drawer organizers and small see-through plastic storage boxes with lids. Work through your pantry and remove food that has exceeded the expiration date. The first time my mother-in-law and I went through my spices I realized that I had three containers of nutmeg (which I hardly use) and several near empty containers of garlic salt. Find a place for each object by grouping like items together. You might have a shelf for canned vegetables and fruits, and another shelf for cereals and bread. Store items like flour, sugar and spices in plastic storage boxes to prevent spills. The storage boxes make packing much easier as you prepare to enter the final phases of your move. Simply put the lids on them and pack them away.

When you arrive at your destination the boxes can be pulled out and placed into your new cupboards.

Neutralize

In the postpartum period following the birth of my youngest son, I decided that our living room and kitchen area needed some color. After several unfortunate painting escapades, we ended up with a cranberry red kitchen and a mustard yellow living room. I loved the walls, but the color explosion wasn't really appropriate for the real estate market. Because we moved within a year of his birth, I found myself cracking open the primer and the beige and tan colors much sooner than I had expected. When it comes to colors and selling your home, stay away from the *commitment* colors. Play it safe by gravitating towards more neutral shades.

Stage

Home staging has become popular in recent years. The basic idea behind this trend is that your house is streamlined and decorated in a way that prospective buyers can easily see themselves living there. In markets where selling is difficult or for homes that have been on the market for several months, staging can work wonders. The cost of staging depends on the size of your home and the area that you live in, but many people who invest in staging report that they were able to recoup the investment through a quicker sale.

If you are like the rest of us and you can't afford to stage

In my mind, my mom was a pioneer of the staging process long before professionals were charging expensive fees to help you sell your home. She made sure that the house was clean and that our personal belongings were tucked away in packing boxes so that potential buyers were better able to imagine themselves living in our home. She and I scrubbed floors together on our hands and knees. We cleared kitchen counters and tossed chocolate chip cookie dough into the oven on low heat before showings

Ultimately, a clean, inviting, neutral home is the goal of staging.

Selling your existing home might be one of the first big challenges that you face when preparing to face a move for medical school, residency, fellowship, or an attending job. Getting your home market ready is the first step. Deciding how to sell your home is the next hurdle.

Using a realtor

Hiring a realtor that you can trust is essential. A good way to find an agent is simply by word of mouth. Ask friends and neighbors to share their experiences with local realtors to help you narrow your choices.

A reputable agent should be honest with you about the condition of your home and any repairs that need to be made. Though it might be a financial necessity to consider the percentage of the price of your home the realtor will earn, it is also important to make selling the house quickly a priority. There was a well-known realtor that we knew during residency who was famous for getting homes sold quickly. She was brutally honest about what needed to be done in the house, and charged one of the highest commission fees. Her tenacious efforts to sell homes quickly usually paid off. As a result, she was a popular choice despite the higher fee.

Selling your house with a realtor can provide you with an added bonus in the unpleasant event that you have to move on for residency, fellowship or that attending position without a sold sign posted in your front yard. If you have established a working relationship with your agent, handling the sale of your home from a distance will be less frustrating. It will be important to communicate by phone and email, but you can relax knowing that your agent is doing everything possible to sell your home.

FSBO (pronounced fizbo)

If the idea of paying realtor fees stirs up bad feelings, you may be considering taking a stab at selling your home yourself. Putting your house on the market For Sale by Owner (FSBO) can sound appealing, but there are a few important things to consider before taking the plunge.

- ✓ If you are working or have small children, will you have the time to devote to advertising and showing your house?

- ✓ Do you have a good enough grasp of the business side of a home sale to complete the transaction?

There may be no harm in trying to sell your home without the help of a realtor. Carefully consider the market and your ability to follow through on all aspects of selling. Several people have been able to successfully sell *by owner* before moving on, but it can be a risky proposition that has the potential to backfire. With the stress of finishing medical school or moving on from residency, adding the extra responsibility of selling your house yourself may be more than you bargained for. Before you make a final decision about whether or not to try and sell your own home, visit these websites and arm yourself with as much information as possible about the process.

Owners

www.owners.com

Owners is a website for individuals looking to sell their home without the use of a real estate agent. Listing your house on their website is free. A premium membership for $377 will provide you with an MLs number. You will then be listed on realtor.com as well as other major websites. This requires the payment of a 2-3 percent commission to the realtor who sells your home.

ForSaleByOwner

www.fsbo.com

Fsbo.com is a paid service for listing your home. Fees range from $69.95- $199.95 for 9 months of listing. There is a flat fee MLs package for $499.95.

ByOwner

www.byowner.com

List your home at ByOwner for a fee. ByOwner will help you appraise the value of your home and the listing is valid until your home is sold.

HomesByOwner

www.homesbyowner.com

At HomesByOwner you can list your house for free with a single picture or pay for package upgrades to allow you to add more features to your listing.

If you decide to try selling your home without the help of a realtor, create a careful timeline for yourself. You will need to determine when the point of no return is when it comes down to being able to independently market your home. If your house isn't sold by this time, it will be important to have a plan B in place.

Chapter 20

Create a moving timeline

Nothing is particularly hard if you divide it into small jobs.
—Henry Ford

With your move to start residency, fellowship or an attending job looming in the not-so distant future, it isn't unusual to feel overwhelmed by the enormity of the responsibility. Packing up your home and moving across the street is stressful. If you have to relocate to another state altogether, the task seems even more intimidating. Break down your move into more manageable parts so that you don't feel overwhelmed by the enormity of what you are about to undertake.

The *Match* process only provides a timeline of roughly twelve weeks for families to accomplish the various tasks involved in the planning and execution of a move to begin training. The timelines presented in these pages can serve as guidelines to help you organize your move.

They are only meant as a way to help you begin to pull things together in your mind. Consider your own schedule and the things that you need to accomplish and put together a plan of attack that best meets the needs of you and your own family.

T-minus 12 weeks

The results of the *Match* are available mid-March. The unintended consequence of this process is that 4th year medical students and their families have a three month window to begin the daunting task of putting together an anticipated or perhaps unanticipated move.

With the buildup to the *Match* still fresh in your mind, it's time to begin the checklists if you haven't already. It can be tough to motivate yourself, but adequate planning trumps flying by the seat of your pants when it comes to moving. Do as I say, not as I do though. Here's a true confession: As my husband's fellowship began winding down, I intended to get into planning mode. I was finishing my master's
thesis though and was so exhausted from managing fellowship, the children and my own

Eight to twelve weeks before moving

- Begin researching neighborhoods to find out as much as you can about the town you are moving to. Contact a local real estate agent to arrange a visit to look at home or rental units.
- If you haven't already contacted an agent locally to put your own house on the market, you will need to take action now. Start getting your house ready to be put on the market and finalize all realtor contracts.
- Talk with your financial institution about getting a letter of preapproval if you are planning on purchasing a home.

attempt at building a career that somehow the deadlines just passed me by. The day that our movers came, I had several loads of laundry that I had meant to finish washing and folding that were still languishing in our clothing hampers.

Ultimately, the movers packed our dirty clothes in my son's *Pack 'N Play* portable crib and put it all on the truck. Plan early and save yourself headache, embarrassment, and laundry to wash as soon as you arrive in your new town.

T-minus six to eight weeks

You know where you are moving for training or the post-training job and the excitement has worn off. It isn't crunch time yet either. This is the period of time where it is easy to to

---

Six to eight weeks before moving

✓ Select a date for your move. What day does your spouse need to begin medical school or residency? Are there any orientation days scheduled that would require you to be there early? Determine a range of days that are realistic for you to travel and leave yourself a little wiggle room if you are driving in case you have car problems or other delays.

✓ Secure a moving company or rent your truck or POD. This is the time to put down your deposit and make sure that you will have a truck or storage unit available for you when you need it.

✓ Begin packing. Packing up a household is a process that can take several weeks. Don't wait until the last minute to get things done or you may end up having to leave things behind or risk not leaving on time.

✓ Purchase airline tickets or plan your travel route. Decide how you are going to move and lock in prices on airline travel before the prices go up.

trick yourself into believing that you still have time to get things done. It is also a little early to work on some of the major packing and home renovation projects that need to be finished before you move on.

I say this with love: *Don't become complacent.*

Yes, I waited to rent our U-Haul truck until just three weeks before our moves between residency and fellowship. Let's just say that organization hasn't always been my strong suit. OK, it still isn't. Obviously, that was not a scenario that I had played out in my mind.

It took us another week to find a moving company willing to pick up our belongings. We were lucky to come across a moving company in the State we were moving to that would be in our area and would lend us some room on their truck. If we hadn't gotten lucky, our move could have become very complicated.

Don't be me. My dad always told me that success is a result of hard work and preparation. I have a tendency to lag behind when it comes to preparing.

> **Four weeks before moving**
>
> ✓ Notify Journals and magazines of your change of address. Keep that New England Journal of Medicine coming each month by notifying the publisher of your impending change of address.
> ✓ Arrange for your utilities to be turned off at one home and turned on at the next. Do this by telephone or for a small fee online. Visit *www.connectutilities.com* for information about getting connected online.
> ✓ Obtain any documents that you will need for transferring to a new school, pediatrician or veterinarian.
> ✓ Have a garage sale. If you are far enough along with your packing and sorting, this is a good time to get rid of items that you won't be taking with you.

T-minus four weeks

The one month mark leading up to a move is a very emotional time for me. It usually is the time of that last girls' night out, last auxiliary club meeting and is when the good-byes begin in earnest. Packing gets ratcheted up a notch and one thing becomes clear to me: We are moving.

This is when I start obsessing about the uncertainties that are facing us. Am I forgetting something important? (Usually yes!) Will we be happy, will the kids make friends, and what will our new lives be like? All of these feelings are completely normal and it is easy to get swept up in them. No. It is easy to become immobilized by the stress and worry.

It is important to remember to take the time to honor your feelings as you continue planning your move and taking care of the necessary details. Don't forget to take some moments for yourself to allow yourself to feel the sadness about moving and the excitement that comes with a new stage in your lives.

T-minus two weeks

When we moved to Florida to start fellowship, we had entered moving crunch time without a moving company during the middle of one last final tough month of call. We celebrated getting it all done as we traveled across the country only to realize that we had forgotten to check one very important item off of our to-do list. We pulled into our new town and then squealed into the first repair shop that we could find. We ended up with an expensive repair bill because our brake pads had worn through and damaged the actual brake shoe.

> **Two weeks before moving**
>
> ✓ Make plans to have your mail forwarded by filling out the paperwork at the post office. This is a good time to send out change of address postcards to family and friends as well.
> ✓ Have your vehicles serviced so that they are road ready. If you are traveling by car, having your vehicle checked out by a qualified professional is imperative.
> ✓ Decide where you will stay once your boxes are packed.

The two week mark signals the point of no return. If you have any unfinished moving business to get done, this is the last opportunity to save yourselves a great deal of stress and frustration. The closer you get to your moving date, the less likely it is that you will be able to finish the many tasks related to pulling together your move.

Hell week

One week before moving

✓   Finish packing the rooms and as much of your kitchen as possible. At this point, you should be living with the bare minimum of clothing and other items that you need to get through your move.

✓   Sort through spices and food and discard or use perishable items. Don't take anything on the road with you that should to be refrigerated or kept in a freezer.

✓   Touch up the walls with paint. Keep some extra paint in case there are any unexpected dings that happen during the actual move, but get the big stuff done early.

✓   Pack travel suitcases. Figure out what clothing, personal and professional items you might need for the time that you are on the road and your initial days settling in. Pack a children's travel case with games and snacks as well.

✓   Find your documents. Make sure that you have all documents associated with your move with you while you are on the road. Set aside your

- Rental Truck Agreement
- Moving Company Contract
- ₊Insurance Information (automobile and health)
- Hotel reservation receipt and airline tickets
- Driver's license and registration documents
- Travel maps or GPS system
- AAA membership (If you don't have one, consider getting one before you move. They will come out and help change tires or tow your vehicle at no cost to you.)
- Credit cards
- Rental agreements or closing documents for your new home.

I'm not trying to be negative. The week leading up to a move though can be an extremely emotional and frustrating time. This is a time of final good-byes, finding documents and is generally speaking when all of Murphy's Laws tend to come into play.

As much as you plan and prepare for you move, many of the most important details need to be left unfinished until this last week. Whether it is the overwhelming amount of work left to be completed or the looming good-byes that are the source of so much stress isn't really important. This is a tough week. Planning in advance for it will help you to approach it in an organized fashion, and knowing what to expect will help you to survive it.

Because I tend to procrastinate, hell week hits me harder than some. I perform well under pressure though, so I suppose that evens things out a little bit.

We moved every few years when I was growing up. I never experienced a move that was easy or where something didn't inevitably go wrong. The final week was always the most difficult for everyone, and pulling together all of the loose threads was stressful.

The best advice that I can give is to accept that things will go wrong. They will be your *moving stories* someday. Even big things that go wrong have a way of working themselves out. Try to relax and enjoy your last few days in your home and with friends and family by taking regular breaks for yourself. Don't forget to plan dinners or coffee breaks with friends, even if those dinners are pizza around the packing boxes.

One Day before your move

The advice that I want to offer up at this point is to simply go and have a stiff drink or two. Not wanting to encourage alcoholism or risk anyone misunderstanding and trying to finish up their last minute details after consuming a few drinks, I'll try to dig deep and find some better advice:

1. Close up all of your final boxes, but leave out one box for any miscellaneous extras that you might need to pack at

the end of the day of moving. This could include cleaning supplies that you are taking with you or your sheets and pillows if you are spending your final night in your home.

2. If you haven't already, pick up your rental truck. If you are moving yourself, make sure that the truck has a full tank of gas and seems to be in good working condition before loading it the next day.

3. Go through each room and plan which room you will start in. Come up with a game plan for how you can best organize the moving day. Pack children's boxes or important items that you will need immediately into the truck last. This way, they will be the first items unloaded from the truck.

4. If you haven't cleaned out your refrigerator and freezer, remove the remaining items and turn it off. Hopefully, you will just need to spray and wipe down the inside after you finish loading the truck.

5. Leave out cleaning supplies if you need to tidy up. Create an area to store paper towels, towels, sponges and any other items that you will need to clean after the boxes are gone.

After you have organized your last day, take time for yourself to relax and try to get to bed early. This is where I would caution against trying to stay up late to get things done, or actually playing drinking games. You will need to be on top of things for moving day, so the best case scenario is that you get a good night's sleep.

D-day

When I was a little girl, my family moved every one to three years. My dad was an officer in the military and this meant that packing up, saying good-bye, and starting over was just the flavor of my life. Moving day represented a final endpoint to me where I tied up loose ends, said good-bye and mentally closed the door on a chapter in my life. There was always a lot of work left to be done, and we dug in as a family to make sure that by the end of the day, we were ready

> ## D-day
>
> ✓ Load the truck systematically. Take your time and insist on regular breaks to prevent injuries. Pack your vacuum last after you have cleaned your carpeting.
> ✓ Sweep floors, wash down counters and clean out the refrigerator. Assign jobs to your spouse and kids and have the whole family get involved in cleaning up before you leave.
> ✓ Do a final walk-through. It's the only way to discover that you have left your digital camera with three months of family pictures saved in it on the window sill.

to move forward. I always left my own room until the very end. While my family was busy finishing up in the kitchen or basement, I allowed myself time in my room to breathe in all that was good about the life that I was leaving so that I could grieve what I was losing, find closure and move on.

Saying good-bye to family and friends is always the hardest part of moving. Moving represents adventure, change and the hopes of fulfilling new dreams, but it also means accepting loss and the grief associated with the ending of friendships as we know them. The people who you feel privileged to know and who have shared your life during this stage of training will be farther away. Say your good-byes to friends knowing that keeping in touch daily is as easy as sending an email, checking in on *Facebook*, or picking up the phone. Things will change, but your friendships can remain strong.

The First Month

Each time I have moved it has amazed me how quickly my new town has become home. I marvel at the fact that weeks earlier I was living a comfortable and familiar life and that this now is identifiably the past. There are new streets to memorize, grocery stores to explore and shopping malls to walk through.

The disorientation never lasts long and as it subsides, I always emerge into a new and familiar normal. The first month after a move is an important transitional period. Be patient with yourself as you navigate your new surroundings, unpack, and adjust to your new life.

> **Starting over**
>
> ✓ Get your new driver's license and license plates. A trip to the Department of Motor Vehicles doesn't sound particularly appealing, but it is better to take care of it before you get pulled over.
> ✓ Enroll children in new school districts.
> ✓ Find a new family doctor, pediatrician, veterinarian and dentist. Since you are new to the community and aren't familiar with the clinics in your area, ask neighbors or nurses in the hospital for recommendations about who they trust with their healthcare needs.

Come up with your own individual moving plan that fits the needs of your move. Remember to be flexible though. If you don't get things done exactly as planned, don't give in to frustration or let it be a further source of stress. Your timeline is a work in progress that is meant to steer you through this transition.

Chapter 21

Planning your move

A journey of a thousand miles must begin with a single step.
—Chinese proverb

As a military brat who can add attending two junior highs and three high schools to her résumé, I can assure you that you never get used to moving. You can learn to accept it, tolerate it, and even plan for or it. Embracing it is a whole other story.

Without a doubt, our most stressful move during residency came when we left Northern Ireland. We had only lived in the United Kingdom for a year. I hadn't anticipated making any close friends during our short stay, but that year was full of surprises. We met a wonderful family that we have continued to have contact with throughout the years. We were also blessed by the birth of our oldest daughter.

I gave birth to our second child a month before our international move to the United States. Because I had failed to pack before she was born, my first post-partum month was punctuated by nursing the baby, chasing my toddler and packing up rooms into boxes. That chaotic experience taught me the value of planning ahead. I was actually busy cleaning the house and finishing up with the final preparations a half an hour before we had to leave for the airport. Forget the fact that my husband was lying on the floor in the guest bedroom reading while I scrubbed the bathroom. I agreed to bury the hatchet, so I'll try not to bring it up again.

Organize a moving company or reserve your U-Haul

Once you have determined a tentative moving date, you will need to consider how you would like to implement your move. If you are accepting a post-training position, your move will most likely be paid for. Moves after medical school or for residents going on to fellowship will come out of your own pocket. Shopping around for the right moving company can be a frustrating experience. Budgets for medical students and residents are often incompatible with the high costs of some of the major moving companies. Although tax-deductible for some, these expenses can simply be out of reach.

Finding a company to orchestrate your move may be as simple as looking in your local yellow pages. Don't overlook small moving companies in the town you are planning on moving to. Often, they are able to offer you better deals than the larger well-known (and more expensive) companies. When we moved for Fellowship, we chose a company from the town that the fellowship program was in. They already had trucks going out during that time and were able to accommodate us by moving us with another household. An interesting twist is that the truck broke down on the highway and we passed it on our way out of town. Take some time to check into your options before making the decision that works the best for your family.

There are several excellent moving resources on the web that can help guide you in the right direction:

MoverMax
www.movermax.com
MoverMax is an excellent website to start with. Here, you can fill out a change of address with the US Postal Service online, have your utilities connected, purchase moving and packing supplies online and find a variety of advice on planning and executing your move.

Moving.com
www.moving.com
This is another excellent moving resource that can help with the planning of your move. Get quotes for self-service and full-service movers after filling in some information about your move, compare your salary with the cost of living in your new community and have some of your utility services connected online.

Physicians Relocation Services
http://physicianonthemove.com
Physicians Relocation Services is a company that was founded by the spouse of a physician. They provide real estate information and realtor services, maps, information about schools and cost-of living for physicians relocating anywhere in the United States.

The obvious answer for many families on a budget is to simply do the hard work of moving themselves. It is possible to rent a truck to fit any household size and unless you are moving an extremely large household, your class c driver's license will be adequate. The costs are minimal and depend on the size of the truck and the distance that you will travel. There are many reputable companies to choose from. For more information about a do-it-yourself move, the following websites are a good place to start:

UHaul
www.uhaul.com
Even if you decide not to use U-Haul for your move, a visit to their website is a must. There you can determine the size of the truck you would need for your household size, order supplies online and find tips to make your move proceed more smoothly.

Penske
www.pensketruckrental.com
Penske is another popular truck rental company. Use their website to calculate the truck size that you will need and order packing materials online

As inviting as the idea of a do-it-yourself move is, consider the reality. The downside of moving everything yourself is that it can be a great deal of work. In addition, driving a van may be an added stress that will serve to compound the frustration of the move. Unless you tow your car behind you or drive separately, one of you will also have to drive the vehicle to your new destination.

The do-it-yourself move can go smoothly, or it can turn into a do-it-yourself disaster. Are you prepared to deal with some of the problems that move-it-yourselfers face, including the truck being unavailable for the time you scheduled it, blown out tires or thick black smoke rising out from beneath the hood? This is especially important to keep in mind if you are moving over a long distance. Be prepared to face any unexpected situations that arise by giving yourself extra time to travel and by keeping your rental documents readily available. When you rent your truck ask what you will need to do if your vehicle breaks down. Be sure and write down that information, and the name of the person whom you spoke with. Keep all of this information with while you travel.

For short distances, moving it all yourself is still likely to be the best option. Keep in mind that many medical families will be looking to rent a truck. Determine what size truck you will need and reserve it as soon as possible. Though it is possible to reserve a truck online, it is in your best interests to take the time to go to the office or make phone reservations if your nearest rental center is too far away. Online reservations can be tenuous and more difficult to hold the company to.

PUD

A popular alternative to the traditional do-it-yourself move involves packing the boxes, loading them into a truck and having someone else drive. Affectionately termed *Pick-up and Deliveries* or *PUDs* by many in the moving industry, these moves can be relatively inexpensive (as moving costs go) and hassle-free. The basic premise of a PUD move is that you pack the house yourself. The moving company will either drop off a trailer for you to fill up on your own, or will arrive on a certain day to help you load. Your goods will be dropped off at your new home on a pre-arranged date. PUD moves are slightly more expensive than traditional do-it-yourself moves, but they can be significantly less expensive than relocating with a moving company.

UPack
www.upack.com
This is a service offered through ABF Freight System, Inc. They offer a PUD style service "You pack, We Drive, You Save". It is certainly worth getting an estimate.

PODs
www.pods.com
Order your POD trailer up to 30 days before your move and take your time loading it. No ramps are needed because PODs are at ground level. The PODs can be stored at a storage facility until you are ready to move. PODs will then move your storage unit to your new location

Movex
www.movex.com
Movex offers self-service moving. You load the truch(they provide everything), and they drive. They are also the only PUD moving company that will transport your vehicle.

WeHaulMoving
www.wehaulmoving.com
Another you pack, we haul, you save website. Self-storage, self-moving, and truck rental are also available.

Some words of caution: When we arranged a PUD move, we packed the house ourselves and arranged to have the company help us load the truck. We neglected to read the fine print in our contract that they would not help us unload. The truck experienced multiple delays and didn't arrive at our home on the established drop-off date (of course). All of our household goods arrived after my husband had begun his internship year. This meant that I was alone at home with our 18 month old and 12 week old when the truck finally arrived. My husband could not leave the hospital and so I had to unload the entire truck by myself while my children waited in the house and the two burly movers sat and watched. They were sympathetic, but insisted that they were unable to help due to liability issues. Despite the back-breaking trauma, I still think that PUD moves are the best way to get you from point A to point B

Chapter 22

Packing up the pieces

The difference between the possible and the impossible lies in a person's determination.
—**Tommy LaSorda**

Packing up the house is absolutely one of my least favorite parts of the moving process. If I were trying to be positive, I'd say it is an opportunity to sift through all of the junk that we seem to effortlessly acquire, but somehow that is little consolation when you are surrounded by boxes, paper, Styrofoam peanuts, garbage bags, and in my case children playing in boxes of Styrofoam peanuts. If you haven't tried to sweep up those peanuts, you are in for a real treat. They are so light that they scatter everywhere, and they are so big that if you try and use a vacuum you have to dismantle the vacuum cleaner to dig out all of the little pieces. So what is the solution to the packing nightmare?

Make a list of the supplies that you will need

This is a great way to take control. Decide what you will need and determine where you need to go to get it. Start a list. You will need:

- ✓ boxes

- ✓ tape

- ✓ packing peanuts . Do yourself a favor. Bubble wrap or packing paper is a much better investment.

and

- ✓ a wide black permanent marker just to get started.

Finding good boxes that are inexpensive or free is something that should also be considered carefully if you are packing up yourself. It is tempting to go to the grocery store for boxes, but often they are not strong enough to hold books or breakables. Electronics stores like *Best Buy*, or retail chains that sell home supplies like *Home Depot* or *Lowes* may be willing to provide some of their sturdier boxes at no charge to you. Don't wait until the last minute. Once boxes are opened they are usually broken down and set aside to be thrown away. As a result, they may not be in good condition anymore. If you are able to wait a week, you may end up with new boxes from their latest shipment. An added bonus may be that you can ask for a certain sized box and have it set aside for you.

Another creative option is to purchase *Rubbermaid* or *Sterilite* storage containers. They can often be purchased for less than the standard cardboard moving boxes or for pennies more. Not only are they more durable than a box, but they are also waterproof and reusable. After the move, they can be used as storage containers for the playroom, garage or attic. This is the route that we chose after one of our boxes filled with family photos suffered water damage in a move. It was in the days before digital photography, and the photos could not be salvaged. To this day, I regret not having the pictures in our albums.

Companies like U-Haul do sell packing boxes. You may first want to get online and do some price comparisons.

Packing Kits
www.packingkits.com
Packing Kits provides you with a box calculator and a home survey inventory form that can be downloaded and filled out to get bids from movers to accurately estimate moving costs. They also sell boxes and other moving supplies.

Fast Cheap Boxes
www.fastcheapboxes.com
At Fast Cheap Boxes, you can calculate how many boxes you will need to pack your house effectively. Purchase boxes, tape, bubble wrap and other moving supplies for less than they would cost at a store. Shipping on all items is free.

Deciding how to wrap and pack your breakables is another issue to resolve. Newspaper can be one good form of packing paper, but the ink has a tendency to rub off onto the items you are packing. Consider whether or not the items can be cleaned before using any paper with newsprint on it and whether or not you want to invest the time and energy to clean them. The best choice is really packing paper designed for moving that can be purchased in stores that sell moving supplies. As a final note, if you are having a moving company do your packing, keep in mind that they will likely not cover any damages if you pack anything yourself.

Choose the room you use the least

Getting started is the hardest part of any big project. To begin the packing, choose a room that you and your family spend the least amount of time in. This might be a guest bedroom, basement or even a home office. My vote is to start in the guest bedroom. Then you have a great excuse for why your mother-in-law can't come by for one last visit. By picking a room that is relatively unused, you will ensure very little disruption in your daily routine. For the most part you will be starting out by packing things that you aren't using frequently. You can gradually work through your home going in the order of importance of an area to your family. Your kitchen should be the last place that you pack.

As the date of the move approaches, you can begin to pack the rooms that you are using. If you have small children, leave one box out for them filled with some well-chosen toys to play with. You will want to leave this box open so that they can play right up until you put it on the truck. When the time to load this box comes, they may even want to tape it up themselves.

Set up a garage sale box and a garbage box

These are the first two boxes that you should bring into the room that you are packing. Line your garbage box with a large, durable garbage bag that you can replace as it gets filled. As you begin the packing process, sort through your belongings and decide what you want to keep, what you would like to put in a garage sale and what can simply be thrown away. Look at this as one of the hidden bonuses of your move. This is your opportunity to clean out those cupboards that you haven't opened in years. You will be able to get rid of your clutter and hopefully make some money in the process.

Label your boxes

This might sound like a no-brainer, but labeling each box as you pack it will simplify the unpacking. Don't wait until after you are done. It is easy to forget what has gone into each box after the room is finished. You may even consider buying different colored permanent markers for each room if it helps with the organization. If you have small children, don't forget to put that permanent marker out of their reach or you may find yourself adding *prime and paint walls* to this list. Again, I'm speaking from experience here. Let me just add that we were so stressed out trying to prime and paint before the walk-through that we ended up knocking over the can of paint and spent an additional few hours cleaning up the spill while the children danced around the empty apartment.

Lighten up

As a rule of thumb, if you cannot lift the box, it is too heavy. This of course does not hold true for things like televisions or other large appliances, but over-packing boxes can lead to injuries, broken boxes, and a lot of frustration. It is hard to be patient when you've been packing for hours, but you are better off taking a break and coming back to it later than straining back muscles trying to lift your boxes during a move.

Books are the worst culprit. When we were moving to the United States, my husband tried to fit all of his medical books into one very large box. He was proud of how quickly he had been able to get them all packed until he closed the box and tried to move it. We had to reopen the box and spend time dividing up all of the books and repackaging them into smaller boxes. By we, of course, I mean me. Also, in an interesting twist, once he packed his books he declared that he had finished packing. Did I promise to bury the hatchet?

When possible, avoid over-packing your boxes. Choose smaller boxes and pack them only as full as you can while still being able to comfortably carry them. If there is still room left in a box that is getting heavy, fill it with packing paper. Large boxes can hold a lot, but should really only be used for bigger, bulkier items or clothes.

Wrap your breakables

Dishes, glassware and other breakables should be wrapped in several layers of paper or bubble wrap to make sure that they don't shift in the box and are protected to a degree from impact. They can be packed in boxes filled with wrinkled wads of packing paper or clothing to add an extra layer that will act as a cushion in the case that the box falls or is damaged in some way. Make sure that there is plenty of space between your breakables so that they remain intact if there is any shifting of the contents. Finally, don't forget to label the box *Breakable* or *Fragile*. If the box needs to be upright, remember to write *This Side Up* on your box as well. Don't rely on your memory. In the wee hours of loading the truck (after pizza and a few beers), this is likely to become a distant memory, and if you have other people helping with the loading, they won't know your intentions.

Stack your boxes

When you finish with a room, stack the boxes on one side of the room, bring garage sale boxes to a designated area in the garage, and throw out your garbage. This will enable you to walk through the rooms and clean or complete projects like touching up paint on the walls. It also will effortlessly organize your garage sale for you. If you are throwing away larger items, call the service that you use for collecting garbage to arrange for a large garbage pickup. Keep in mind that items like old computers can't be thrown away. The lead in the computers presents an environmental hazard. You will have to pay a few dollars to have them disposed of properly.

Don't neglect the finer details

Whether you are leaving a rental or turning over a beloved home to a new family, you will want to give yourself time to clean and do any touch-ups before moving on. This is always part of that final push during the last days, and it has spelled disaster for me more than once. There was the time when my husband was finishing residency when he had to work right up until the day that we moved. We had two toddlers and a newborn and we needed to touch up the walls in the townhouse we were renting. I overestimated my ability to balance the task of caring for our children with the work left to be done. Late in the afternoon, after nursing the baby and getting him back to sleep, I tripped over a can of white paint. It spilled out all over the basement floor. I exhausted all of our paper towels and cleaning rags, and was still working on sopping it up when the rental agent arrived for the walk-through. If it hadn't been for my kind next-door neighbor, I wouldn't have managed to get it cleaned up at all. Of course, there was also the time that we were leaving a rental house after fellowship and we accidentally had our lights turned off too early. I cleaned into the evening using flashlights. Fortunately, I finished the vacuuming earlier in the day and it all worked out. Clearly, I have learned my lessons the hard way.

Cleaning up the house and taking care of paint touch-ups is a detail that many people forget to plan for. It's an important detail that can also take longer to finish than people realize. I know that after a hard week of finishing the packing, loading a U-Haul, caring for children and preparing for a move, that the last thing on my mind was cleaning out the refrigerator or scrubbing the toilets. It is the right thing to do though, whether you are renting or have sold your home, so you will have to dig in for that final push.

Plan it

Survey the house to see what work needs to be done. If you make an effort to write it down as you are packing, you will save yourself time and frustration in the final hours of your move. Go through each room of the house and note any cleaning, paint touch-ups, or repairs that have to be done before you move on. This will also give you time to purchase paint, brushes and other cleaning supplies that you will need. Don't forget to set aside:

- ✓ small bucket

- ✓ sponges and cleaning rags

- ✓ towels for wiping down surfaces

- ✓ paper towels

- ✓ cleaning sprays for the kitchen, bathroom and floors

- ✓ a sponge mop for the floors

- ✓ a vacuum cleaner

Make a note of any supplies that you will need and have them ready in advance.

Do it

Don't wait for the boxes to be neatly tucked away on the truck to get started on the work that needs to be done. It won't be possible for you to clean out the freezer or refrigerator or finish the bathrooms, but with a little work, you can take care of the bedrooms and other living spaces so that when it comes to pulling it all together there is less work to be done. Work through rooms, living areas and the garage in the weeks and days leading up to a move and leave the bathrooms and kitchens until the end.

- ✓ bathtubs and sinks

- ✓ toilets

- ✓ refrigerator and freezer

- ✓ stove and inside of the oven

- ✓ cabinets

The final thought that I will leave you with is that everything will take you longer than you think it will. Everything. Take it from the girl who cleaned out the refrigerator into the wee hours of the night after spending a day loading a truck and cleaning from room to room during one particularly stressful move. Plan extra time for cleaning and start as soon as you have a room packed. Waiting until the last day to get it all done will leave you overwhelmed and exhausted.

Chapter 23

Garage sale advice

Even if you're on the right track,
you'll get run over if you just sit there.
—Will Rogers

With most of the move organized and ready, you can turn your attention to that final garage sale. If you have consistently set aside garage sale boxes as you packed, you will have an organized group of boxes ready to be unpacked in your garage and set up for a sale. Plan to have your garage sale no later than two weeks before your move. This will give you time to finish packing, make arrangements for a large garbage pickup, and take any items that did not sell to Goodwill or another charitable organization.

Choose a time

Choosing a good time for your garage sale depends on the area that you live in. In many communities, Saturday is the big sale day, but in Minnesota, Thursdays and Fridays are reserved for garage sales. I have lived here for more than ten years, and it still feels wrong to me. Most garage sales start between 7am and 9am and go into the early afternoon or evening hours. Check your local newspaper to get a better idea. Regardless of the time that you plan on starting, recognize that you will have early birds out eager to get a bargain as early as 6am. Decide how you want to handle that in advance.

When we prepared to move after fellowship to begin our lives post-training, we planned to start our sale at 8 a.m. At 5.30 in the morning, someone actually lifted up our garage door and started going through the tables of items in our garage. By the time I had thrown some clothes on and headed out into our garage, two more cars had stopped. I was shocked by the idea that people would simply open our garage door and go through our things. Even more interesting to me is that a woman came back by the house later to pay for items that she had taken while I was sleeping.

Organize with other spouses

If there are several families in your area getting ready to move on to the next phase in their medical careers, a group or neighborhood garage sale is a good way to bring in more potential customers. As an additional bonus, it also provides you with a final opportunity to talk with other spouses who are experiencing the same stress and anxiety about moving that you are. Knowing that you are not alone and that other people are experiencing similar doubts or fears can be very validating.

It may even be a good idea to pick a central location for the sale and then help other spouses to bring their sale items from home. You can split the cost of renting a U-Haul before your sale and work to pick up as many loads as you possibly can. That might be a tall order in the days before a big move, or it may be just the distraction from the chaos in your home that you need.

The only words of caution that I can offer are to avoid shopping at your multifamily sale. I have a hard time passing up a bargain and when we took part in a residency garage sale at the end of training, I came home with several items that I didn't need and ultimately had to get rid of before we moved.

Get the word out

Advertise your sale in the local newspaper or community website. If your neighborhood association permits it, prepare bright signs with bold lettering to hang on streets near your sale. Put the signs out the evening before the sale to draw even more traffic. The signs should be easy to read and should point potential shoppers in the direction of your house. I'm sure it goes without saying, but once your sale is over, be sure and take your signs down.

Get organized

Your tables should be arranged so that the merchandise is easy to find. Group similar items together at the same table to keep each area organized. For example, if you are selling baby clothes put them on one table and sort them by size to make things easier for your potential customers. In addition, wash and touch up clothing items with an iron to get the best prices (Or if you are like me, press them with your hands while you fold them. Who has time to iron clothes?). Larger items like furniture, bicycles and appliances should be set up so that they are easily visible from the street. It is often the big ticket items that attract shoppers. Once customers stop and approach the garage, they are much more likely to look at the smaller items that you have. To get the best prices, make sure to clean and dust all furniture and household items. Get rid of any dirt by wiping down all of your furniture and knick knacks. You can even touch up scratches on wooden furniture by investing in wood-finish pens that matches the stain on your furniture from your local hardware store. When we were moving on for fellowship, we put our old worn out coffee table into the sell pile. After using a wood finish pen and polishing the table, it looked so nice that we decided to keep it.

Chapter 24

Moving on

When one door of happiness closes, another opens; but often we look so long at the closed door that we do not see the one which has been opened for us.
—Helen Keller

After we moved to start my husband's residency in internal medicine, I was miserable. There is just no other way to say it. During his internship year, I felt isolated, lonely and like I just didn't belong. I was struggling to raise our 1 year old and our newborn on my own without family or friends nearby to offer help or companionship. My husband, on the other hand, had walked right into an established group of fellow residents and attending physicians. He was working hard each day, but he never ate lunch alone and the opportunity was always there for him to bounce questions or problems off of his peers. For him, a big challenge might have been learning an interesting and important procedure. In moments of self-pity, I often lamented that a big day for me was going to our area *Wal-Mart* and eating lunch with the kids in the cafeteria there. Some days, my biggest challenge was making sure that we left the house with diapers or that my children had on socks that matched. I loved being a stay-at-home mom, but I was lonely.

It took me a little over a year to find my groove and start to feel like I fit into the community and had friends and acquaintances that I could turn to for play dates, political debates or the odd mom's night out. During our first year there, I had counted the days until residency was over, adamantly insisting that I couldn't wait to leave. As our final year approached, I desperately wanted to slow time down. I was counting down the days, but instead of being happy about leaving, I felt sad. When we left for fellowship after three years, I cried. No one was more surprised about that than me.

Settling in, making friends and assimilating into the community is by far the most difficult part of moving. In the chaos and stress of planning a move, it is also the most over-looked aspect. We tend to concentrate on the actual move itself, feeling relieved when the moving company has finally delivered all of our goods to our new home for us to unpack. What we often fail to plan for is the inevitable time that comes after the move when we are adjusting to a new community and are looking to build a new support system for ourselves. Once the boxes have been unpacked and the new driver's licenses have been issued, many spouses go through periods of isolation and loneliness and can struggle to fit in to their new communities. This can be exacerbated for the stay-at-home parent who has to work much harder to get and meet other parents and children.

As a general rule of thumb, from someone who has moved at least seventeen times in her life, I can confidently say that it takes at least a year to begin to feel comfortable in a new community. Establishing friendships can take even longer depending on your age, the ages of any children that you may have, and whether or not you are employed. I found it easier to transition from one community to another when my children were preschoolers because parents were more likely to meet each other during the children's activities. Many older children are dropped off for sporting events and practices and meeting parents can take longer. Working outside the home is also a good way to establish a social network more quickly.

It seems like it is easier for the medical student or resident to adjust to the changes after a move because they begin working and quickly establish a daily routine. They develop professional and social relationships with colleagues and have the added benefit of continuing to plan their next career move. As spouses, we are often left on our own to adjust and settle in to the new community. Feeling lonely or overwhelmed is an understandable reaction to this big change. It is important to be patient with yourself and recognize that adapting to any major life transition takes time. To help you adjust, consider the following suggestions:

Explore the community

Forget about just finding the grocery store or the local *Barnes and Noble*. Get your hands on a copy of an area travel guide and discover as many fun and inexpensive things to do in your community as you can. The biggest surprise that I discovered after moving to Minnesota is that we have beaches. There are more beaches for me to explore and swim at in the summer here in Minnesota than there were when we lived in Florida. Finding the area attractions will help you feel more connected to your community and as a bonus, it is a fun way to chase away boredom.

Be sure and contact the Chamber of Commerce for your new city to get as much information as you can. To find information for your local Chamber of Commerce, visit the national Chamber of Commerce website.

> **U.S. Chamber of Commerce**
> **www.uschamber.com**
> The US Chamber of Commerce website provides a directory of all US Chambers by State and City. A wealth of information is available about schools, churches, employment, community and business.

The more involved you become in your community, the more quickly it will begin to feel like home.

Join MOPs

For mothers who are staying at home or are looking to connect with other mothers, Mothers of Preschoolers (MOPs) is a valuable resource. MOPs is an international organization that caters to both stay-at-home moms and working parents. They hold weekly meetings in communities nationwide and also offer the opportunity to connect online.

> **MOPs**
> **www.mops.org**
> The MOPs website provides a variety of resources for moms looking to make connections with other moms. Find a local group, visit the discussion forums or browse through their online MOPs University if you are interested in taking online bible courses.

Take a class through community education

Most cities have community education programs with classes for children and adults. Sign up for cooking class or an informational session on budgeting or gardening. Pick an area of interest to you and then jump in with both feet. Chances are good that you will meet some like-minded individuals that you may end up going out for coffee with and slowly getting to know.

Join a book club

Look to your area book stores or local library to find out about any book clubs that are currently active and are accepting new members. This is a great way to meet other people and keep your mind active. I have been a member of a local book club for two years now. I'm embarrassed to admit that in all of that time, I have only actually managed to finish one book in time for a meeting. Though I was an avid reader in high school and college, the demands of five children usually take precedent over any reading time that I might have. I will sheepishly admit that I have gone from trying to read the books to . . . reading the book reviews online to . . . distracting from the fact that I haven't read the books by talking about the dessert. Fortunately for me, my book club members still invite me back every month. It has been a fun way to find out what people are reading, meet new friends and taste great homemade desserts.

It's important that you get out and work at meeting other people in your community. This can be really hard to do, especially if you are shy, are feeling depressed, or you have small children at home. Take your children to the park, walk through the neighborhood, or even go to the area fast food restaurant with a play area and talk to other moms while your children play. The more involved you become in your community, the more quickly it will begin to feel like home.

Get involved in the medical spouse alliance

If there is an alliance group associated with your spouse's residency program, pony up the annual fee and attend the meetings even if you aren't a joiner. The only reason that I initially got involved in the medical guild during residency was to be supportive of my husband. I rolled my eyes about the meetings, complained about the lack of organization or failure of volunteers to show up, and protested the fact that we were forced to wear nametags with our name and our spouse's specialty on them.

"I am my own person, not my husband's career", I would complain to a friend that I had made at one of the meetings. She would agree and the rumblings about call schedules would ripple across from the other side of the table. We would laugh, connect and pretend to be annoyed by it all. At the end of the night, my husband would ask me how it was. I insisted it was a waste of time, but heaven forbid my babysitter would actually cancel and I was unable to go. In all honesty, I enjoyed the meetings and spending time with other medical spouses. The key was that I was meeting people. Some of them I got along with and some of them I didn't (but hey, that just kept things interesting). The important thing is that I was reaching out and getting to know other men and women who were experiencing a similar time in their lives.

The Appendix contains a detailed list of various medical spouse alliance organizations throughout the United States. If your state or program is not listed, contact the residency program's Department of Medical Education to find out whether or not there is a spouse support group at your program. If no spouse group is available, taking the initiative to start one may be the best way of all to get to know others who are going through the residency experience with you.

Part Six
Surviving Call

*The worst thing in your life may contain seeds of the best.
When you can see crisis as an opportunity, your life
becomes not easier, but more satisfying.*
—Joe Kogel

I still vividly remember preparing for residency and listening with dread to the stories of spouses that were already deep in the trenches of training. I couldn't imagine spending thirty six hours (or more) without my husband. The thought of moving across the country to start a journey full of unknown challenges made me break into a sweat. I was overwhelmed by a sense of impending doom when it came to discussions about residency or fellowship.

I wish I could tell you that I faced each of the challenges that residency and fellowship handed me with grace and poise. Unfortunately, that isn't the case. Like many medical spouses struggling to balance rough call schedules and family life, I grappled with periods of unhappiness and grief. During the years that my husband completed his training, I brought three children into the world, earned my master's degree, suffered the loss of my grandmother and went through the unexpected death of a good friend. Often as a function of my husband's schedule, I rejoiced alone . . . and cried alone. As a result, I grew bitter and angry. I felt unhappy during the hard months, and I struggled to cope. I still cringe when I think about my reactions to some of the challenges that we faced during training. I have come a long way.

It took me a long time to work through my resentment and to begin to embrace our lives. When I look back on the training years now, I realize that we had many good memories. It was just difficult to acknowledge the good times when we were overwhelmed by the demands of training. When I was finally able to stop wasting my energy resisting residency, I began to accept the training lifestyle and even found joy in our day to day.

Finding a place of peace with training is a process. Residency and fellowship will change you each day. You can choose the direction that you take, and at any time on the journey you can change the course that you are on. If I can do it, you can too.

Chapter 25

Anticipating stress

Every path has its puddle.
—English Proverb

My husband and I had a huge argument after our fourth child was born. He was on call and had to go in and see a patient and I was busy at home with our children. My two month old had discovered that if he cried, I would pick him up. I couldn't get anything done. The dirty clothes were bursting out of the laundry room, the kitchen sink was full of last night's dinner dishes and the family room looked like a toy store had exploded in it. I had just applauded myself for managing to get dressed when my husband came through the door.

"I don't have any t-shirts", he said while looking at my piles of clothes to be folded.

I explained that I had t-shirts of his and that I would have them folded after the kids got to bed, and this seemed to placate him . . . until he walked into the kitchen.

"I thought you were going to clean up the kitchen", he chided.

To say that I was feeling defensive would be an understatement. The hairs stood up on the back of my neck and before I could take a deep cleansing breath to address the issue with composure, I lashed out at him. I was tired and had spent the day taking care of the children. I hadn't even made it into the shower. Within minutes, we were knee-deep in an argument. This all could have been avoided if we had simply taken the time to talk about what we each needed and what we could realistically accomplish, but we were both too exhausted to step back and address the issues rationally.

Stress is an unavoidable side-effect of having a busy life. The pressure associated with learning how to treat people who are sick and who are depending upon you to make them well is enormous. Supporting someone who is working in a demanding profession can also be very difficult. This is heightened if you have your own career or are at home with small children. When we allow ourselves to become overwhelmed by stressful situations we can end up taking our feelings out on the people who are most important in our lives. We might yell at our spouses or become impatient and irritable with our children. Some people deal with stress by detaching themselves from family members, which can only serve to increase the burden of stress for everyone.

One of the best ways to avoid becoming overwhelmed by a situation is to take control of it before it happens. Even in the midst of crushing stress, it is possible to take charge and turn things around. Take control of your situation by anticipating stressful triggers in your life, determining a plan of action and following through.

Anticipate stress

My husband and I had to eventually sit down and discuss the fact that there would be changes in the household with the new baby here. I was able to tell him how difficult it was for me to get things done and how tired I was. He understood that we just might be living out of the laundry baskets for a few months. This wasn't what he wanted to hear, but because he knew in advance that when he came home from work the laundry might still be in the baskets and the dishes might not be in the dishwasher he was able to accept this and respond by folding laundry with me or putting away the clean dishes instead of reacting with disappointment.

Before a difficult rotation, take some time to talk together about what will be going on in your lives that month and discuss ways to problem-solve before you are in the thick of things.

Is there a family engagement to attend? Hammer it out before the month gets started whether or not you will both be able to attend, and then lay it to rest.

✓ Do you have a deadline for work or school? Find childcare in advance to ensure a positive outcome.

✓ Are their birthday or anniversary celebrations coming up? Use the call schedule to plan parties or nights out in advance.

✓ Will your spouse be working long hours this month? Come up with some solutions together to help you get through the days.

Of course, the best laid plans can fall apart, so it is also important to be flexible. It's frustrating when the call schedule or *post-call* exhaustion puts a kink in our meticulously scripted plans, but in the long run it is better to accept the situation and come up with a plan B.

Anticipating stress also means recognizing what your partner's hot button issues are and agreeing to avoid them. The middle of a busy Q3 month probably isn't the best time to bring up the fact that your friend who is married to a teacher lives in a beautiful house with a picket fence while you are stuck renting a townhouse. For me, comments about the kitchen or the laundry are off limits, especially when I am on my own trying to take care of our children. Asking me how my diet is going while I'm eating a cookie is right up there on the list too. As a compromise I have to try really hard not to criticize him for spending too little time with the children when he is busy.

Anticipate that your spouse will be MIA.

Don't plan your four year olds' birthday party and expect your husband to make it home from rounding on the weekend to help you deal with fourteen screaming four year olds. You will only be setting you both up for disappointment and frustration. How do I know this? I planned my daughter's fourth birthday party during what was a very busy month for my husband. He warned me that he might not even make it home from the hospital in time, but I hedged my bets and just *knew* that he would make it home eager and willing to help out. The outcome of this debacle was obvious to everyone but me. When all was said and done, I had seventeen children and one large and excited Australian Shepherd celebrating in my house. I put our dog in the backyard and turned my attention to the children. Within thirty minutes all of my party games had been played. The children wanted to go outside and I eagerly let them out in the backyard while I put the candles on the cake and stopped to just catch my breath.

To make Murphy and his laws proud, the dog did her business when I let her outside and several of the children stepped in it. I ended up taking off all of the children's shoes before they had cake. When the parents arrived to pick their cherubs up, they had just settled down to watch a *Blue's Clues* video while I cleaned the bottoms of their shoes up with an old tooth brush and soap. My husband just shook his head with an *I told you so* look.

I felt resentful that my husband had not been able to make it home. After all, we couldn't be expected to put our lives and the childrens' birthdays on hold until after training was over. This wasn't how I had imagined that life would be. My expectations were unrealistic and it was hard for me to accept that this was the life that we had both signed up for. I could have anticipated that my husband would not make it home, invited fewer children, chosen a different day or asked a friend to come over and help me. Certainly this would have alleviated some of my stress. I had set myself up to feel resentful about our situation and angry with my husband. As an even more interesting twist, my husband had felt resentful of my choice. He had spent his afternoon rounding on critically ill patients worrying about the party and regretting not getting home sooner.

It is important to accept that your spouse's time will be limited and to plan around their schedule as best you can. This might also mean having a friend come over to help with a birthday party (and taking a lot of pictures for mom or dad to look at later) or postponing certain activities until a less stressful rotation.

Anticipate that you will feel tired and lonely sometimes

This is true whether you are working outside of the home or are busy at home with your children. You will be the one responsible for keeping things running at home. If you are a stay-at-home parent, you may find that your conversations are limited to talking about Bob the Builder ("Can he fix it? Yes, he can."), or that you are exhausted from keeping up with the daily chores of maintaining a house as well as the additional responsibilities of calling the exterminator and the plumber on the same day. That is a true story too. It involves some very creepy looking, monstrous, cockroach-like Palmetto bugs and a two year old who managed to get the television remote control to flush down the toilet.

Determine how you best cope with this kind of stress and what you can do to make things easier for yourself. Does calling your best friend or your mom help you to maintain your sanity? Buy a calling card each month for $20 and use every penny on it without adding to the financial stress of training. If working out will help you regain your sanity then by all means join a gym or start taking brisk walks each morning. Do what you have to do to keep yourself feeling ok.

Anticipate that your spouse will be exhausted

After our first child was born, I got a taste of what my husband went through during call. Within a few days I had become irritable and short-tempered. One day when our son was just a few weeks old, my husband offered to watch him while I went to the mall for an hour or two. The baby had woken me up multiple times during the night to nurse. I felt like I hadn't slept at all. I was so tired and overwhelmed that instead of enjoying the time to myself I ended up finding a pay phone in the mall and I called my husband crying. In retrospect, I realize that I was only getting a few hours of sleep and that I was feeling very stressed out and incompetent in my new job as a mother. New motherhood parallels residency in many ways. Your spouse will be getting very little sleep and will be under a great deal of pressure to learn new procedures and to stand up to the scrutiny of their peers.

My husband was able to recognize that I needed a break in those early days and the greatest gift that he gave me was a few hours to myself. Even now, sixteen years later, if I'm not getting enough sleep and am feeling out of sorts, he will send me out to Barnes and Noble. That is exactly what I need in order to feel better. When my husband is tired, the only thing that helps him is getting sleep. I have learned to recognize this in him and I do my best to let him lie down and rest for a few hours.

The relentless stress and sleep-deprivation during clerkships and residency makes it more difficult to catch up on sleep, and with both partners feeling stressed out and exhausted, coping skills can suffer.

Recognizing that lack of sleep exacerbates existing communication difficulties is a big step. Talk with your spouse about what they need to help them get through a tough call month. Would a catnap after work help refresh him? Would sleeping in one morning on a weekend improve her overall mood? Try it out and then assess how effective it was. As you navigate those early months of call, you will discover what works best for you both.

Don't forget to assess your own exhaustion. Being the do-it-all spouse can be very draining. Pencil yourself into the plan as well. If you need a morning to sleep in, ask for it. Take steps to ensure that you are able to be well-rested and as relaxed as possible too.

Chapter 26

Twenty-five things to do
on a call night

*Times of stress and difficulty are seasons of opportunity when
the seeds of progress are sown.*
—Thomas F. Woodlock

I loved call nights when we lived in the United Kingdom. The
hospital system that my husband worked for provided residents
with call suites. These came equipped with a kitchen, living room
and several bedrooms. At one smaller hospital, only one internal
medicine resident took call each night. This meant that when he
was lucky enough to cover that hospital we had the entire suite to
ourselves. Each call night, I brought up food to cook in the
kitchenette. We watched television in the living room interrupted
only by his pager. There were enough bedrooms that our youngest
was able to sleep comfortably. My husband and I each had a

room as well. Our experience that year was rare, but it was also the source of many pleasant memories from training.

Most of the time, call is experienced as a shockwave that builds with intensity as the month drags on. Hearing "I have ICU this month" during residency was enough to send me into orbit when my older children were babies. It went beyond the struggle that I personally experienced as a new mom learning how to balance a family's needs. I wanted my husband around. I missed him and I felt cheated out of time together as a couple and as a family. I didn't always handle it well because I spent the time feeling angry and exhausted. As fellowship got underway, I discovered an uncomfortable little secret: Call nights could be times for me to take care of myself and my own needs. Planning my call night extravaganzas filled me with a guilty pleasure.

You won't be able to change your spouse's call schedule, but you can take control of how you feel in their absence and nurture yourself at the same time. The list of things to do on a call night is endless. Here are twenty five ways to embrace the positive in the ugly face of call:

Paint your toenails

Pamper your feet by adding bath oil to a pot of boiling water. Try chamomile, lavender or lemon oils. If your feet feel tired and worn out, a good peppermint oil will soothe away the discomfort. Create your own personal foot spa by pouring your soaking solution into a pan that will accommodate your feet. Soak your feet for as long as you want. Give yourself a pedicure and then pull out the nail polish. Spice things up with red or go for a subtle pink. Make the experience about pampering yourself.

Celebrate a movie night

Pull out all of the stops and pick out the movies that you have been dying to see but are just not of interest to your partner. For me this meant marathon nights of Lifetime movies, *Beaches*, and

Awakenings once the kids were tucked in. Plan your Netflix list with the call schedule in mind or take a trip to your local video store. Do the popcorn, candy, and soda and enjoy a fun date with yourself.

Call your best friend

If phone calls to close friends tend to take a while, use a call night to catch up on the latest gossip or goings on without your spouse tapping his watch and wondering when you are going to finally get off of the phone so that he can spend some time with you.

Start a new book

Fill the tub up with warm bubble bath, grab a cup of tea and a brand new book and spend the evening catching up with your favorite author. Lose yourself in a book without feeling guilty about finishing laundry, cooking a nice meal or cleaning up. If you are like me and having children has stripped you of your ability to focus on any text longer than a reader's digest article, try listening to a book on tape as an alternative.

Organize your kitchen drawers

If knowing that there is a place for everything and that everything is in its place is comforting to you, by all means tackle those kitchen drawers. My linen cupboard looks like a bomb went off in it and I can live with that (and with two teenagers in the house it's a good thing that I can turn a blind eye) but my kitchen drawers are a sore spot for me. They get cluttered when I feel like my life is cluttered (and when the kids rummage through them). Spending an hour or two sorting through them can be great therapy for me.

Bake Homemade Bread

Forget the bread machine. Kneading, pounding and shaping bread yourself is all a part of the therapeutic bread baking experience. Try out innovative new recipes and be prepared to go off of your low carb diet for the evening.

> **Bread Recipes**
> Visit **www.cookingbread.com** for innovative ideas and free online baking classes.

Paint a room

There is no easier way to make a change to the walls without dissent than to paint them when your spouse has call. Actually, I wallpapered once and it took my husband two days to notice. If you have children, make sure that they are tucked into bed before you get to work. My most infamous painting story involves me painting the walls with kids underfoot. The entire can of paint got knocked onto our white carpet. I grabbed the wet-dry vacuum from the garage and the kids all took turns bringing me pitchers of warm water to pour onto the paint so that I could vacuum it up. I got every drop of paint out of the carpet and then turned to see that the garage vacuum had sprayed paint all over the wall and our sofa. I think I need to leave painting to the professionals.

Exercise

Burn calories and boost your mood by starting a call night exercise program. Dance to a Richard Simmons video (I really did own a copy of *Sweatin' to the Oldies*), walk or jog on your treadmill, take the dog for a long walk outside, or ride your bike. Take care of yourself by getting into better shape and burning off some of your negative feelings.

Rent your favorite TV series and watch the season from beginning to end

Have you gotten behind on *Desperate Housewives* episodes? Do you wish you could watch the first season of *Cagney and Lacey* that is now out on DVD? TV therapy can be a great way to boost your mood. When my husband was doing fellowship, I tucked the kids into bed, got on my own pajamas and snuggled up under the covers for marathon catching up sessions. Go to your public library, buy some used DVDs at Amazon.com or rent the series from *Netflix*. Enjoy the time to catch up on your favorite shows.

Learn how to sew

If you have access to a sewing machine, try your hand at making children's clothes, table runners, curtains or your own fashion accessories. Enjoy learning a new skill. Once you have mastered the art of sewing, you just might be able to earn a little money on the side selling your products online or at craft shows.

Try out a new recipe

I started subscribing to a German cooking magazine years ago. When my husband had call, I loved trying out new recipes and sharing them with my neighbors. Some recipes turned out to be smashing successes and others, well . . . let's just say that my neighbors were polite but they didn't ask for seconds. I enjoyed trying out new things and getting the kitchen good and messy without worrying about my husband coming through the door and stressing out over the mess.

Catch up on your ironing

Ironing is not my cup of tea. Quite frankly, I would rather clean out the bathtub or steam clean the carpets than pull out my ironing board. My mother-in-law, on the other hand, finds ironing relaxing. If ironing is a calming activity for you, and you love the instant gratification of watching a wrinkled shirt transform into a crisp blouse, by all means use a call night to get caught up.

Start a blog

Share your experiences and opinions in a public or private blog online. Blog anonymously about politics or residency, or use your blog as a way to keep

Free Blog Sites
www.blogger.com
www.wordpress.com

family and friends updated about your life. Either way, writing out your thoughts and feelings can be an effective and entertaining way to express your feelings.

Color your hair

If you feel like you need a change, consider trying out a new hair color. Obviously, this is not a suggestion that everyone can embrace. If you haven't colored your hair before or are trying out something new, use the non-permanent hair colors. These colors usually wash out after ten to thirty washings so if it doesn't turn out exactly like you hoped, the agony will be short-lived. If you are like me, skip this suggestion altogether and leave anything related to your hair to the professionals.

Learn a foreign language

Have you always wished you had taken French in college? Would learning Spanish help you professionally? Make call nights your foreign language nights. Invest in some inexpensive language CDs and workbooks or borrow them from your library. Devote call nights to learning vocabulary and grammar. As you become more proficient, look for videos that you can rent and watch in your language of choice. Many DVDs out on the market today now allow you to watch the movie in Spanish. We purchase our German movies through Amazon. Whatever your choice, enjoy the experience.

Teach yourself to dance

You might not have the money to take a dance class, or you may feel uncomfortable with the idea of beginning a ballet class offered through Community Ed, but you can learn the basics and build

Fun Ballet Videos

Ballet Class for Beginners
by David Howard

New York City Ballet: The Complete Workout

Ballet Boot Camp
by Jesica Sherwood

The Ballet Workout
with Melissa Lowe

your confidence in your own living room dance studio. Who needs a professional dance bar when the back of the sofa will provide you stability . . . and a soft place to land when you are tired or ready for a break.

Learn to play an instrument

If you always wanted to learn how to play the guitar or your french horn from high school is collecting dust in the attic, consider Q3 call the opportunity to practice uninterrupted every third night for a month. If you have never played, pick up a copy of the *Teach Yourself to Play* series from your local music shop or online bookstore and begin working on learning to read music and play the right notes.

Learn how to quilt

A friend turned me on to quilting during residency. I'm not gifted with a sewing machine and my quilts are never square, but throughout the years, I have created keepsakes for my husband and children that I hope they will always treasure. I have to admit that I've also become a closet fat quarter addict. I have enough fat quarters stashed away in my work area to make a quilt for everyone that I know. I have grown to love the look and feel of certain fabrics.

Enjoy a girl's or guy's night out or in

Pick a night to catch up with friends during a tough call month. Invite everyone over for a pizza and movie night or meet at a restaurant for dinner. Connecting with friends will pull you out of your slump and you will be able to refocus on the positive things in your life. When I started going out with some of my medical spouse friends once a month, it felt like I was finally able to breathe again. I came back feeling refreshed and with a renewed sense of purpose.

Explore local museums

Take a trip to a nearby science or art museum or spend a day exploring your museum of natural history. For an interesting deviation from the run-of-the mill museum experience research small, unique museums in your area. Maybe you live near the Mt. Horeb Mustard Museum in Wisconsin or are within driving distance of *The Museum of Bad Art* in Dedham, Massachusetts. Take advantage of the local culture.

Take up knitting

Buy some beautiful yarn, a set of knitting needles and a copy of *Knitting for Dummies* and then get to work on your first pot holder or scarf. This is a relaxing way to de-stress and the added bonus is that you can get an early start on your holiday gifts.

Knitting Online
Join Ravelry and become a member of an online group of knitters who share their experience and and love of all things yarn. They also have a forum for medical spouses.
www.ravelry.com

Take an art class

Find an outlet for you to express yourself and get in touch with your inner artist by signing up for a class in watercolor, pottery or working with charcoal. Turn your home into your own personal art gallery during residency training.

Expand your home improvement skills

Take a class at your local home improvement shop and learn how to tile the bathroom floor, use a scroll saw or frame out a wall. Much area home building mega centers offer in store and online clinics and workshops for budding do-it-yourselfers. Get online at www.homedepot.com and watch videos about installing flooring, creating a home theater, installing toilets and faucets and more.

Make your own jewelry

If you are patient and have an eye for detail and fashion, get hooked on learning how to make necklaces, earrings and bracelets. There is a wide variety of glass, wooden and ceramic beads to choose from. Some people become so involved in this trendy hobby that they even make and paint their own unique ceramic beads.

Learn to yodel

Take voice lesson and learn to sing (or yodel if you must). Use call nights to break out the karaoke machine, crank up the music and sing your heart out. I was lucky enough to inherit the family piano when my parents moved, and so I spent endless hours singing and wishing that I had practiced my piano enough when I was younger to actually be able to accompany myself. Invest in an inexpensive keyboard to help you with the notes and enjoy learning the art of singing.

Now that I have gotten the ball rolling, come up with twenty five more ideas for things that you can do when you are struggling through tough call months or just to keep your head afloat during residency training. Keep your list handy so that when you are feeling overwhelmed or sad you have something to help you plan your time.

Chapter 27

Here on planet earth

Time marks us while we are marking time.
—Theodore Roethke

Your four year old pulled the sofa cushions off and they are lying on the floor. Your one year old scattered the clean and folded laundry throughout the living room while you put another load into your washer and there are half-crunched cheerios littering your dining room floor. In order to get anything done, you are sacrificing sleep. (Okay, I'm describing the state of affairs in my house. I assume your house is clean and that you are stumbling over these lines in horror.). The idea that you can just kick back and pamper yourself on call nights while the walls come crumbling down around you sounds appallingly naive. Finding a way to inject some fun into the hard work that comes with raising children, moves for training and the stress of call schedules will help you feel more balanced and positive though, and ultimately it will ease the stress and help you to cope.

It is understandable and completely normal to be feeling frustrated by toxic call schedules and overwhelmed by the unpredictable nature of the lifestyle. I have dined alone at a booth in a fancy restaurant on our anniversary while my husband answered page after page in the lobby. My grumblings during residency about certain rotations or attendings probably resonated throughout his entire program. I truly wanted to be positive. I later wished that someone had shaken me by the collar and told me to get it together during the early years of residency training. Come to think of it, someone probably did, but I was too busy feeling sorry for myself and wishing things were different to pay close attention.

Looking for the positive in a difficult situation doesn't invalidate the effort, sacrifice and struggle that can sometimes overcome us during the training years and beyond. It took me years to realize that I had to create my own happiness. Medical training will pass whether you do your best to embrace the time or you are dragged kicking and screaming the whole way. How you ultimately choose to cope with the stress and uncertainty can change you as a person. I wasted several years feeling unhappy before I was able to accept our lives and feel good about the choices that we made. During times of negativity, I felt cynical and pessimistic and those characteristics distanced me from family and friends. Finding that inner peace was a process that I decided to embark on when I realized that life was happening and I was missing it.

Take charge of the medical training years so that when training is over you will not look back with regret about that time in your life. There are no do-overs. This is it.

Cut back

Are you trying to accomplish too many things? It is great to be room mom or to volunteer in the schools to help with the Book

Fair or Teacher Appreciation Day activities. Are you also trying to work part-time, take a college class and prepare fancy meals each night? I am a doer too. Unfortunately, in our exuberance to take on new and interesting challenges, we can lose sight of the fact that ultimately it is impossible to do many things and do them all well. Eventually, I get burned out and I start feeling resentful. Reduce the number of things that you are trying to accomplish to a manageable and realistic level. Go back to school when your kids are older or agree to volunteer occasionally at your kids' schools instead of weekly. It's ok to lighten your load so that you can make time for yourself.

Share your feelings

Talk about what you are going through with a trusted friend, fellow medical spouse, minister or therapist. Allow yourself to feel angry, and be honest with someone who will support you and understand what you are going through without being judgmental. Putting on a glass smile each day when you are feeling bad isn't healthy. It's ok to vent to a trusted friend when times are hard.

Let it go

I know, I know . . . this is so much easier said than done and it usually involves so many deep breaths that it can border on hyperventilation. Develop the ability to move forward and walk away from your negative feelings once you have shared them. Months of Q3 call can be grueling, but don't let it make you miserable. I am a reformed pessimist, so I know of what I speak. If I can turn things around and start to see the silver lining, anyone can.

Count your blessings

When times are tough, it is easy to forget what is good in our lives. Stop yourself when you have a negative thought and focus on the blessings that you have even if it feels awkward or forced. Be thankful for your health, your home, your children, your pets, your parents or the friends that you are close to. Once you turn your attention away from the things that are upsetting you and focus on what is good about your life, you will feel better about where you are and what you have. With practice, appreciating the positive things in your life will become automatic.

Switch gears

If you are feeling overwhelmed by the things that you can't control, turn your inner spotlight onto what you can. You can't control the fact that your spouse is doing a grueling general surgery residency, or that you had to leave a good job to move. You can, however, control whether or not you are exercising or taking care of yourself. You are in charge of deciding to go back to school, helping children with homework and your own attitude and appearance. Changing how you perceive residency training can make a big impact in your feelings in general. Replacing negative thoughts with positive ones and focusing on what you have control of will help you to feel more balanced and your life more manageable.

Nurture yourself

At the top of your list of things to do each day should *be take care of myself.* If you aren't nurturing yourself and making sure that your needs are met, you will be exhausted and you eventually will feel burned out. Go back over the twenty-five things to do on a call night and decide to make room for yourself and your needs.

With busy call schedules often dictating routines, it often feels like your basic needs take a back seat. Don't neglect yourself. Though at first glance it might seem that using call nights to take care of your needs is unrealistic, recognize them for the opportunities that they are. Let the cheerios lie on the floor, leave the laundry unfolded and concentrate on your needs.

You deserve it.

Epilogue

The medical training years are a journey. During residency and fellowship, we often joked about just making it through to the light at the end of the tunnel. The end of training was just the beginning of a new chapter in our lives though. It took my husband and I nearly two years to decompress and find ourselves in each other again after training was over. Finding a more solid financial footing took almost seven years. After the excitement of starting a new post-training job, buying a new house and celebrating the end of fellowship was behind us, we were forced to look at what was missing in our own lives as individuals and as a couple. The stress of living a life on high alert where we were simply struggling to put out fires and make it to the next step took its toll on us and our family.

As you approach the end of training, be realistic about your expectations for each other. Celebrate the success of finishing residency and be kind to yourself and to each other while you navigate this new phase of your journey.

We are now more than nine years out of training. Since fellowship ended, we have welcomed two new babies into our home, have moved twice, and have battled with our own health issues. During my pregnancy with our fifth child, I was diagnosed with a mediastinal lymphoma. After spending years supporting my husband through medical training, my husband and I found ourselves in the unenviable role of patient and caregiver.

It was during that time that I was able to finally lay my bitterness over the training years to rest. Being at the other end of the pager gave me a sense of gratitude and peace over the path that we had taken.

Thank you for doing the hard job of supporting your spouse and your family during these difficult years of training. Your sacrifices are a gift to all of the patients and their families.

Appendix 1
Glossary of Terms

Attending: A physician who is finished with residency training and is working in a post-training position.

Call: During the end of medical school and the duration of residency, physicians in training take overnight shifts in the hospital that are referred to as call. Often, the resident will go to work in the morning, stay at the hospital and work all night and then come home sometime the following day.

Clerkships: Clinical rotations that are made during the third and fourth years of medical school. Medical students begin taking call during this time.

Fellowship: After a physician has completed the required residency training in their filed, they may choose to specialize. Fellowships are additional years added to the training process and are usually 1-3 years in duration beyond residency.

Internship: The first year of residency training is referred to as the internship year. Often, this is remembered as the most difficult year.

Match: The process of matching 4th year medical students with a residency position is referred to as *The Match*. Medical students apply to residency programs, interview, and then put together a rank order list of desirable programs. Most applicants are matched with programs in March and begin residency in July.

Q2/Q3: The frequency of a call schedule is often designated using the letter Q. Q2 refers to a schedule that requires a resident to work overnight call every second night. Q3 means that they schedule is for every third night. Though Q2 call schedules are technically no longer allowed (aka. illegal), some programs manage to get around this.

Residency: Following medical school, physicians are required to have clinical training in order to practice as a doctor. Common residency programs include family practice, internal medicine, pediatrics and surgery.

USMLE: The United States Medical Licensing Exam is a test that grants a license to practice medicine in the United States. The test is divided into parts I, II and III. Medical students take the basic science exam (Step I) in their second or third year of medical school. The clinical science portion (Step II) is usually taken before graduating from medical school. The clinical skills assessment (Step III) is taken after graduation.

Appendix 2
Medical Spouse Alliance Organizations

National Organizations

The following resources are for alliance organizations with a national membership base. You do not have to be a resident of any state in particular to become an active member of these organizations.

AMA Alliance
www.amaalliance.org
The AMA Alliance is the proverbial Mother Ship to many State and County alliance organizations. It was founded in 1922 and since that time it has grown into an organization that supports medical families and promotes health through advocacy programs and active participation in legislative policy. Their anti-violence SAVE program is well-known throughout the country. Membership for medical student and resident spouses is $10/yr.

American College of Osteopathic Family Physicians
http://www.acofp.org/Membership/ACOFP_Auxiliary/
330 E. Algonquin Road, Suite 1
Arlington Heights, IL 60005
Toll Free: (800)323-0794
The ACOFP supports residents and physicians through fundraising activities and their detailed advocacy activities in Washington D.C. that promote medical liability reform and positive change for patients and physicians.

The international Medical Spouse Network
www.medicalspouse.org
The international Medical Spouse Network (iMSN) has been active since 1999 as an online support network for the spouses of medical students, residents and attending physicians. It has evolved throughout the years to become a non-profit organization that helps spouses find help and connect with other medical spouses around the country.

The Auxiliary to the National Medical Association
http://www.anmanet.org
8403 Colesville Road, Suite 920
Silver Spring, MD 20910
(301) 495-3779 (ANMA)
(301) 495-0042 (NAAYI)
The national Medical Association Alliance reaches out to regions on a national level to support the National Medical Association and promote issues of health and education.

Southern Medical Association Alliance
http://www.smaalliance.org
The SMA is an organization focusing on the future of medicine. They have a New Physicians Travel Benefit Program that offers medical students and residents the opportunity to stay with host families while interviewing for training positions or jobs. In addition, physician families also donate frequent flier miles to further help struggling new physicians. Membership in the SMA is free.

Organizations by State

The following list of resources categorizes medical spouse auxiliary and alliance programs by state. The list represents an extensive search to uncover as many organizations as possible. Despite this fact, the list is not an exhaustive resource. Organizations without web addresses or that were not searchable do not appear here. To have your alliance contact information appear in updated versions of *Surviving Residency*, or to report website address changes, please contact me through my author website at **kristenmath.com** or join *the Surviving Residency FaceBook* page and report the information in the forum there.

Alabama

Jefferson County Medical Society Alliance
http://www.jcmsalabama.org/content.asp?id=403104
The JCMSA is an organization dedicated to health education. They take part in a variety of health fairs and education workshops and have a separate Resident Spouse Alliance which provides social activities for the spouses of resident physicians. Resident and student spouse membership is only $10 annually.

Madison County Medical Alliance
www.mcmalliance.org
3330 L and N Dr SW # I
Huntsville, AL 35801-5349
(256) 881-7321
The Huntsville area Madison County Medical Alliance is the support organization for the Madison County Medical Society. Annual dues are $75.

Medical Association of the State of Alabama Alliance
www.masalink.org/alliance
P.O. Box 1900
19 South Jackson Street
Montgomery, AL 36102-1900
(334) 954-2500
Toll Free: (800) 239-6272
The Medical Association of the State of Alabama Alliance
www. masalink.org/alliance
The motto for the MASAA is "Dedicated to improving the health of the people of Alabama and supporting the family of medicine". The organization works with the Medical Association of the State of Alabama to promote health education and preventative medicine.

Alaska

Alaska Medical Alliance
www.aksma.org/members.asp
The AMA is a statewide organization of medical spouses affiliated with the Alaska State Medical Association. For membership information, contact the Alaska State Medical association at: *4107 Laurel Street Anchorage, Alaska 99508*
(907) 562-0304
Email: amsa@alaska.net

Arizona

Arizona Medical Association Physician Spouses and Life Partners
www.azmed.org
The Arizona Medical Association is not currently hosting a page for their physician spouse organization, but they do provide updates and contact information in their community events and activities section.
810 W. Bethany Home Road
Phoenix, Arizona 85013
(602)246-8901
Toll Free: (800) 482-3480

Arkansas

Arkansas Medical Society Alliance
www.arkmed.org
P.O. Box 55088
Little Rock, AR 72215
(501) 224-8967
Toll free: (800) 542-1058
Logon to the Arkansas Medical Society website to find out more information about their active alliance organization. They have a variety of community oriented programs to get involved in, including their Reach out and Read program. Dues are $10/year for medical student and resident spouses.

University of Arkansas Resident Spouse Auxiliary
http://www.uams.edu/gme/support_groups.htm
9909 Catskill Road
Little Rock, AR 72227
The Resident Spouse Auxiliary has established itself as a support group for the spouses of resident and fellow physicians at the University of Arkansas. They offer a variety of social and philanthropic activities for all interested members. Annual membership is $25. Childcare is provided at the monthly meetings.

California

California Medical Association Alliance
http://www.cmaalliance.com/
1201 J Street, Suite 300
Sacramento, CA 95814
(916) 551-2028
Toll Free: (800) 492-4054
E-Mail: alliance@cmanet.org
The California Medical Association Alliance acts as a central hub for 15 County alliance organizations. They are active in health promotion through anti-smoking campaigns and legislative policy advocacy.

Fresno-Madera Medical Society Alliance
www.fmmsa.net
The FMMs is active in the community to promote public health and safety. They recently joined forces with the Fresno area Community Emergency Response Team and the Medical Reserve Corp to help educate the community about disaster preparedness.

Los Angeles County Medical Association Alliance
www.facebook.com (search for LACMA Alliance)
The Los Angeles County Medical Association Alliance offers the opportunity to get involved in legislative efforts and community service projects in the Los Angeles area. They have small groups that also get together to play cards, discuss books or work on craft projects too.

North Valley Medical Association Alliance
http://www.nvmaa.clubexpress.com/ *PO Box 994553*
Redding, CA 96099-4553

The NVMAA has been active since 1950. They work on funding for community health grants as well as a healthy lunch and lifestyle program for Shasta County.

Santa Clara County Medical Association Alliance
http://www.sccmaa.org/
700 Empey Way
San Jose, CA 95128
(408) 998-8850
The Santa Clara County Alliance focuses on improving healthcare through education and legislative support for policies.

Sierra Sacramento Valley Medical Association Alliance
http://www.ssvmsa.org/
The SSVMSA actively supports the community through volunteer work, funding of grants to improve healthy living and scholarship programs for health professionals. They also organize social events for medical spouses and their families.

Sonoma County Medical Association Alliance
www.scmaa.org
Post Office Box 1388
Santa Rosa, CA 95402
alliance@scmaa.org
The Sonoma County Alliance is made up of spouses at all stages in their lives. They emphasize "building healthy communities" and fund community grants. Spouses can also take part in quarterly coffees as well as a book club.

Colorado

Colorado Medical Society Connection
http://www.cmsconnection.org/
The Colorado Medical Society Connection strives to support the entire "medical family" by including medical students, residents and attending physicians as well as medical spouses. They have established play groups, book clubs and a wide variety of social activities to support medical families and also take part in legislative advocacy and community health projects.

Connecticut

Yale Medical Partners
http://groups.yahoo.com/group/YaleMedicalPartners Yale
Medical Partners supports the spouses of medical students and
resident physician through social gatherings, playgroups and
family events.

Florida

Alachua County Medical Society Alliance
http://bellsouthpwp.net/s/y/syfert/
Formerly known as the Woman's Auxiliary to the Florida Medical Association, the ACMSA continues to focus on promoting healthy living within the community while helping spouses to forge friendships through monthly meetings and a variety of activities.

Collier County Medical Society Alliance
http://www.ccmsonline.org/
1148 Goodlette Road North
Naples, FL 34102
(239)435-7727
The Collier County Medical Society seeks to support medical families as well as the greater community. Members can take part in playgroups, book clubs and ladies nights out.

Duval County Medical Society Alliance
http://www.dcmsonline. org/alliance/index.htm
Medical Spouses in Jacksonville, Florida can join the active DCMSA to become a part of supporting the Duval County Medical Society.

Florida Medical Association Alliance
http://www.flmedical.org/Layout_1Column.
aspx?pageid=3051
The FMAA is the central alliance for the state of Florida. They are active in patient advocacy as well as providing support for medical spouses and families.

Lee County Medical Spouse Alliance
http://www.lcmsalliance.org/
The Lee County Medical Spouse Alliance offers spouses of

members of the Lee County Medical Society the opportunity to get to know each other better through dinner clubs, play groups, book clubs, walking clubs and more. Monthly meetings take place in area restaurants. Annual dues are $115.

Orange County Medical Society Alliance
http://www.ocms.org/Alliance/default.aspx
901 North Lake Destiny Drive, Suite 385
Maitland, FL 32751
The OCMs participates in community service projects as well as legislative efforts on issues significant to the medical community. Their members span all ages and stages and they work to provide support to each other by working on group projects and activities.

University of Florida Junior Medical Guild
http://jrmedicalguild.blogspot.com/
The UFJMG is a support group for spouses of medical and dental students, residents and fellows. Members enjoy being part of a social club with playgroups, a dinner club and regular monthly meetings. Information about the organization can be best obtained through the UF General Medical Education office at this time._**http://housestaff.medinfo.ufl.edu**

Georgia

Bibb County Medical Alliance
http://www.bibbphysicians.org/alliance.htm
Bibb County Medical Society
770 Pine St. Suite 150
Macon, Georgia 31201
(478)743-5215
The Bibb County Medial Alliance provides opportunities to get to know other spouses while working toward community projects and on legislative issues that affect the medical profession.

Medical Association of Georgia Alliance
www.mag.org/alliance
1849 The Exchange
Suite 200
Atlanta, GA 30339
(678)303-9284
The Medical Association of Georgia Alliance provides support to physician spouses while advocating for physicians and patients and providing community education on healthcare issues. Membership is $25/year.

Kristen M. Math

Idaho

Idaho Medical Association Alliance
http://www.idmed.org
P.O. Box 2668
305 West Jefferson
Boise, ID 83701
(208) 344-7888
The Idaho Medial Association Alliance is the support arm for the Idaho Medical Association. It's educational and charitable activities are supported by six county alliances in Kootenai-Benewah, Southeast Idaho (Pocatello area), Southwest Idaho (Twin Falls area), Burley-Rupert, Nampa-Caldwell and Idaho Falls. Visit the IMA website for more information.

Illinois

Illinois State Medical Society Alliance
http://www.isms.org/affiliates/alliance/Pages/default.aspx
20 N. Michigan Ave.
Suite 700
Chicago IL, 60602
312-782-2099
alliance@isms.org
The ISMSA is active in their role of creating educational programs to fight domestic violence. Their community health advocacy programs are far reaching and include AIDS education, adolescent sexuality and teen suicide prevention.

Sangamon County Medical Society Alliance
http://www.scmsdocs.info/scmsa/
The SCMSA provides physician spouses with the opportunity to make friendships while supporting the goals of the Sangamon County Medical Society Alliance. They are very active in the community and many volunteer opportunities are available.

Indiana

Indianapolis Medical Society Alliance
http://imsonline.org/alliance.php
631 East New York Street
Indianapolis, IN 46202
(317) 639-3406
Visit the IMSA website to find contact information for joining the Alliance and getting involved in their philanthropic activities. They also have active bowling, bridge, gardening and investment clubs for members to be involved on a social level.

Indiana State Medical Association Alliance
www.ismanet.org/alliance
(317) 261-2060
Toll Free: (800) 257-4762
The Indiana State Medical Association Alliance works in partnership with the Indiana State Medical Association. Opportunities for community service and legislative advocacy are among some of the benefits of membership.

Iowa

Iowa Medical Society Alliance
http://www.iowamedical.org/alliance/default.cfm
1001 Grand Avenue
West Des Moines, IA 50265
(515) 223-1401
The Iowa Medical Society Alliance is an official support organization for the Iowa Medical Society. They offer support to medical families as well as opportunities to get involved in health education programs.

Medical Partners
http://www.iowamedicalpartners.com/
Medical Partners
P.O. Box 1612
Iowa City IA 52244-1612
medical_partners@hotmail.com
Medical Partners is the spouse support organization for the University of Iowa Hospitals and Clinics. They have their own website forum and provide information about the local area, housing and member businesses.

Rock Island County Medical Society Alliance
http://qcmso.com/rialliance.htm
201 West 2nd Street, Suite 604
Davenport, IA 52801
(563) 328-3390
The RICMSA provides support for medical spouses through their social events and meetings. A variety of volunteer service projects are available and members are invited to participate in educational opportunities for personal growth. Annual membership is $85 and is due by Jan 1st of each calendar year.

Kansas

Kansas Medical Society Alliance
http://www.kmsalliance.org
The KMSA focuses its efforts on AMA Foundation, health promotion, legislation and membership. Visit their website to find more information about joining or to access the website for members.

Medical Society of Sedgwick County Alliance
http://mssca.com/
1102 South Hillside
Wichita, Kansas 67211
Join the MSSCA to get involved in their healthy communities initiatives or meet other medical spouses from the greater Wichita, Kansas communities.

Kentucky

Kentucky Medical Association Alliance
https://www.kyma.org/content.asp?q_areaprimar
yid=14&q_areasecondaryid=41
4965 US Hwy 42, Suite 2000
Louisville, Kentucky 40222
(502)426-6200
The KMAA website is buried deep within the Kentucky Medical Association website, but it is worth searching for. They provide detailed descriptions of the philanthropic and social activities for the group as well as information about county alliances.

Greater Louisville Medical Society Alliance
https://www.glms.org/Default.aspx?PageID=263
The GLMs Alliance holds monthly meetings for its members so that they can become more involved in social and volunteer activities. Their social groups are varied and include antiquing, book and dinner clubs as well as movie and coffee or lunch bunch. In addition, the Healing Place, Helping Hand and the hospital's Hospitality House.

Louisiana

Jefferson Parish Medical Society Alliance
http://www.jpms.org/index.php?option=com_content&vie
w=article&id=123&Itemid=122
4937 Hearst Street, Suite 2B
Metairie, LA 70001
(504)455-8282
The JPMS in New Orleans supports the Jefferson Parish Medical
Society. They work to raise awareness of local medical and
community causes. Membership is $75/year.

LaFayette Parish Medical Society Alliance
http://www.lpms.org/about-us/alliance-society
Lafayette Parish Medical Society
P.O. Box 51905
Lafayette, LA 70505-1905
(337) 232-2860
The LPMS is an organization promoting health education
and charity. They also offer monthly social activities for their
members.

Louisiana State Medical Society Alliance
http://www.lsms.org/cms/lsms-alliance
The LSMSA works with the Louisiana State Medical Society to
address community health issues in local communities through
health fairs and the distribution of educational materials. They are
the parent organization to the following parishes: Avoyelles,
Calcasieu, East Baton Rouge, Jefferson, Lafayette, Morehouse,
Orleans, Quachita, Rapides, Shreveport, St. Tammany, Tangipahoa,
and Terrebonne.

Orleans Parish Medical Society Alliance
http://www.opms.org/index.php/about-opms/omsa
3600 Prytania Street, Suite 44
New Orleans, LA 70115
(504)891-1288
The OPMsA can be contacted through their website or the OPMs for information about their social and community activities.

Maryland

Frederick County Medical Society Alliance
http://www.facebook.com (search for alliance website) The
FCMSA supports the Frederick County Medical Society. They
have established a program of giving through donations of goods
and services to the needy people of Frederick County and are
active in community education programs.

Med Chi Alliance to the Maryland Medical Society
http://www.medchi.org/alliance
1211 Cathedral Street
Baltimore, MD 21201
(410)539-0872
(800)492-1056
The alliance to Med Chi supports eight local chapters throughout
the state. They are involved in community education, advocacy
and leadership training programs.

Montgomery County Medical Society Alliance
http://www.montgomerymedicine.org/alliance.html
15855 Crabbs Branch Way
Rockville, Maryland 20855
(301)921-4300
The MCMSA supports the Montgomery County Medical Society.
Dues are $90/ year and include membership in the county state
and national AMA Alliance. Their service projects include skin
cancer awareness projects, help for abused and neglected
children and the promotion of internet safety.

Johns Hopkins Medical Auxiliary
www.jhmaonline.org

The Johns Hopkins Auxiliary is a well-established support community for spouses of medical students, residents and fellows at Johns Hopkins University. Their website provides a detailed member-to-member resource guide for newcomers to the area and their interest groups meet several times throughout the month.

Massachusetts

Massachusetts Medical Society Alliance
http://www.massmed.org/AM/Template.cfm?Section=M
MS_Alliance1&Template=/TaggedPage/TaggedPageDispl
ay. cfm&TPLID=92&ContentID=25045
Massachusetts Medical Society Alliance
860 Winter Street
Waltham, MA 02451
Toll Free: (800) 322-2303 X7017
The MMSA supports the AMA Foundation, works on legislative issues affecting healthcare and is involved in community health campaigns.

Michigan

Genesee County Medical Spouse Alliance
www.gcmsalliance.com
The GCMSA is an active alliance that works on community fundraising activities as well as legislative issues that affect quality health care. Their most recent donations were to the local free medical clinic. They were able to raise $500,000 in five years.

Ingham County Medical Spouse Alliance
www.icmsalliance.org
120 W Saginaw St.
East Lansing, MI 48823
(517) 336-9019
The Ingham County Medical Spouse Alliance is a support organization for spouses. They are also actively involved in legislation issues affecting medical education.

Kent County Medical Society Alliance
http://www.kcmsalliance.org/
233 East Fulton, Suite 222
Grand Rapids, MI 49503
(616) 458-4157
The KCMSA motto is "Building a healthy community through philanthropy, advocacy and friendship" and they accomplish this through their active role in promoting public health.

Michigan State Medical Society Alliance
http://msmsa.org
120 W. Saginaw Street
East Lansing, MI 48823
(517)324-2505
The MSMSA is a large active voice for the Michigan State Medical Society. Members have a variety of opportunities to get involved in healthcare legislation, and community health education.

Midland County Medical Society Alliance
www.mcmsa.net
The Midland County Medical Society Alliance celebrates medical families and supports the local community through health education and various outreach projects.

Muskegon County Medical Society Alliance
http://www.mcmsa.org/
The Muskegon County Medical Society Alliance is involved in a variety of projects which encourage community health education and literacy.

University of Michigan Resident Support Network
http://sitemaker.umich.edu/umichrsn/home
If you are looking for monthly meetings, playgroups, family fun nights or to enjoy an evening of wine and cheese with other resident spouses, the University of Michigan Resident Support Network is the place to go. The organization also has philanthropic projects that they work on for the Children's hospital.

Washtenaw County Medical Society Alliance
http://sites.google.com/site/wcmsalliance/home
3031 West Grand Boulevard
Suite 645
Detroit, MI 48202
(313) 874-1360
The WCMSA works hand in hand with the Washtenaw County Medical Society to support public health programs and the medical family.

Wayne County Medical Society of Southeast Michigan Alliance
http://wcmssm.org/wayne_county_medical_society_wcmssw_alliance.htm
3031 West Grand Boulevard
Suite 645
Detroit, MI 48202
(313) 874-1360
The WCMSS works with the Michigan State Medical Society Alliance and the Wayne County Medical Society. They also support the YWCA Interim house by providing food, toys, toiletries and other essentials.

Minnesota

Minnesota Medical Association Alliance
http://www.mnmed.org
1300 Godward St. NE, Suite 2500
Minneapolis, MN 55413
(612) 378-1875
The MMAA supports the Minnesota Medical Association through its educational efforts about the risks of smoking, drug abuse and obesity. As an organization, they promote a feeling of camaraderie through civic action.

Mayo Families' Connection
http://mfc.mayofams.org/
Spouses of residents and fellows at Mayo Clinic can join Mayo Families' Connection to build relationships with other spouses. The MFC provides a wide variety of activities to spouses including an art and culture club, book club, Bunco group, girl's night out, gourmet club and much more.

Side by Side
www.sidebyside-rochester.org
Side by Side is a Christian support group for wives of medical students, residents and attending physicians. They meet weekly and offer prayer groups and bible studies.

Mississippi

Mississippi State Medical Association Alliance
http://www.msmaonline.com/MSMA/Alliance/Alliance_.as
px
P.O. Box 2548
Ridgeland, MS 39158-2548
(601) 853-6733
(800) 898-0251
The MSMAA is the official alliance to the Mississippi State Medical Association. For more information about membership and alliance activities, visit the website to find contact information.

University of Mississippi Resident's and Fellow's Spousal Alliance
http://umcsa.blogspot.com
The University of Mississippi Spousal Alliance is a support organization for the spouses and children of residents and fellows. They organize play groups and monthly meetings to encourage friendships and a support network.

Missouri

Green County Medical Society Alliance
http://www.gcms.us/content.aspx?page_id=22&club_id
=461978&module_id=82122
1200 E. Woodhurst, D200
Springfield, MO 65804
(417) 887-1017
The GCMS alliance is a support network for the spouses of physicians in Green County. They also engage in a variety of community health education activities.

Missouri State Medical Association Alliance
http://www.msma.org/mx/hm.asp?id=Alliance
113 Madison Street s P.O. Box 1028
Jefferson City, Missouri 65102
Toll Free: (800) 869-6762
The MSMA provides opportunities to get involved in volunteer work within the community as well as health education. Members support the Missouri State Medical Association Alliance as well as the AMA Alliance.

Nebraska

Lancaster County Medical Alliance
http://www.lcmaonline.org/
The LCMA supports the Lancaster County Medical Society. They promote health education and research activities and support charitable endeavors.

Nebraska Medical Association Alliance
http://www.nebmed.org/Template.aspx?id=176
233 South 13th Street
Suite 1200
Lincoln, Nebraska 68508-2091
The Nebraska Medical Association Alliance is the official auxiliary organization for the Nebraska Medical Association. They have 10 alliance organizations established throughout the state to support medical spouses.

Nevada

Clark County Medical Society Alliance
www.ccmsa-lv.org/
2590 E Russell Rd.
Las Vegas, NV 89120
(702) 739-9989
The Clark County Medical Society Alliance is an official branch of the Clark County Medical Society. They offer a variety of volunteer opportunities to members interested in getting more involved in helping in their community. Regular membership is $80/year. Resident and medical school student spouses pay only $25.

Washoe County Medical Society Alliance
www.awcmsreno.org
3660 Baker Lane
Reno, Nevada 89509
(775) 829-1303
The Washoe County Medical Society Alliance is a network of medical spouses from the Reno, Nevada area that focus on educational and charitable work in the community. They support their members through playgroups, a book club and other mini-interest groups as well as their regular meetings.

New York

The Medical Society of the State of New York Alliance
http://mssny.org/mssnyip.cfm?c=i&nm=Alliance
865 Merrick Ave.
Westbury, NY 11590
(516) 488-6100 ext 396
The MSSNYA is an avenue for spouses interested in supporting the Medical Society's goals for legislative changes to improve healthcare delivery. The state organization supports county alliances including Broome, Jefferson, Richmond and Schenectady counties. The alliance is involved in several regional conferences as well.

Strong Housestaff Auxiliary
http://www.urmc.rochester.edu/education/graduate-medical-education/index.cfm
Visit the University of Rochester General Medical Education website for a link to the Housestaff Auxiliary newsletter. There, you will find detailed information and calendars about upcoming auxiliary events as well as information about how to join. Annual dues are $15. Members enjoy a variety of social activities for adults and children.

North Carolina

North Carolina Medical Society Alliance
www.ncmsalliance.org
P O Box 27167, Raleigh, NC
27611-7167
(919)833-3836, x132
Toll Free: (800) 722-1350
Members of the North Carolina Medical Society Alliance are invested in advocating for better public health in the state of North Carolina. The headquarters is in Raleigh, North Carolina, but they support several local county alliances.

Greater Greensboro Society of Medicine Alliance
http://ggsma.org/blog/
P.O. Box 4451
Greensboro, NC 27404
The Greater Greensboro Society of Medicine Alliance is affiliated with the North Carolina Medical Society Alliance Health Education Foundation, Inc. They work to improve the quality of healthcare and health education for residents in Greensboro. In addition, the grant some educational scholarships and provide grants for community health projects. In addition, they have moms groups and a book club for interested members.

Mecklenburg Medical Alliance and Endowment
http://www.mmaeonline.com/
The Mecklenburg Alliance is a non-profit organization that advocates health and quality of life for residents of Mecklenburg County. Members have the opportunity to volunteer for to get involved in health-related, charitable, and educational projects.

Medical Alliance of the Piedmont
http://mapws.shutterfly.com/
The Medical Alliance of Piedmont of physician spouses from the Forsyth, Stokes, Davie, Surry and Yadkin Counties. Membership is open to medical student, resident and attending spouses.

Triangle Medical Spouse Alliance
http://trianglemdspouses.blogspot.com
Spouses of residents at the University of North Carolina and Duke University are welcome in the social and service organization. The TMSA has active play groups as well as a variety of social activities to meet the needs of their members. In addition, they participate in a variety of fundraising activities to support community organizations.

Wake County Spouse Alliance
www.ncmsalliance.org/wcmsa.htm
Join the alliance in Wake County to become more involved in activities in your area. Visit their website and read their newsletter, *MDConnection,* to learn more about the organization.

Winston Salem Resident Spouse Association
http://www.rsawakeforest.com/
P.O. Box 15351
Winston-Salem, NC 27113-0351
Spouses of residents and fellows at Wake Forest Baptist Medical Center support each other through group meetings, social, playgroups and volunteer opportunities within the community.

Ohio

Cincinnati's Resident Spouse Association
http://cincinnatirsa.blogspot.com/p/about-rsa.html
The RSA of the University of Cincinnati is a social networking support organization for the spouses of Residents and Fellows. They are actively involved in community projects including the Ronald McDonald House and Toys for Tots, but also endeavor to build social networks among medical families.

Columbus Medical Association Alliance
http://cmaafranklinco.blogspot.com
The CMAA was established in 1940 as a philanthropic and social organization for physician spouses. They continue to win awards for their community health projects.

HOWA
www.orgsites.com/oh/howa/
The House Officer's Welcome Association is a support group for the spouses and families of the University Hospitals of Cleveland. They offer a free Insider's Guide to Cleveland, monthly social events as well as play groups for parents with small children.

OSMA
http://www.osma.org/about-osma/affiliated-groups-and-committees/alliance
The Ohio State Medical Alliance is a support arm of the Ohio State Medical Association. For more information, visit the contact information at their website.

Stark County Medical Society Auxiliary
http://www.scms-a.org
4942 Higbee Ave NW, Suite L
Canton, Ohio 44718
(330) 492-3333
The SCMSA is a charitable organization that supports the Stark County Medical Society through charitable initiatives. They work to foster relationships between medical families through meetings and local events.

Summit County Medical Alliance
http://summitcountymedicalalliance.org/
The SCMA is a medical spouse support organization that also focuses on community health education and encourages volunteerism.

Oklahoma

Oklahoma County Medical Society Alliance
http://www.ocmsalliance.org/
The OCMSA works with the Oklahoma Medical society to promote medical and health education. They also help foster a sense of community for medical families through monthly meetings and volunteer activities. Members can get involved in a variety of special interest groups including Bunco, Mommy and Me, Movie and Lunch clubs and more.

OU Medical Student Alliance
http://oustudentalliance.blogspot.com
Join the Oklahoma University Medical student Alliance for Bunco, movie nights or to join their running club. This organization encourages social networking amongst medical families in training.

Oregon

OHSU Resident Family Network
http://orfn.wordpress.com
The OHSU Resident Family Network is a social and support network for medical families. They encourage support and friendship through playgroups, book clubs, monthly meetings and fun nights out.

Oregon Medical Association Alliance
www.theoma.org/Page.asp?NavID=40
11740 SW 68th Parkway, Suite 100
Portland, OR 97223
(503) 619-8000
The OMAA works on programs dedicated to improving the health and quality of life for the people of the state of Oregon. Spouses of members of the OMA are granted automatic membership. The organization supports alliances in Benton, Clackamas, Douglas, Jackson, Josephine, Klamath, Lane, Southwestern Oregon, and Washington Counties.

Southwestern Oregon Medical Society Alliance
http://www.theoma.org/membership/member
ship-sections/oma-alliance
The SOMSA is an organization of physician spouses who are dedicated to promoting health education. Visit their website for contact information.

Pennsylvania

Berks County Medical Society Alliance
http://www.berkscmsa.org/
1170 Berkshire Blvd
Wyomissing, PA 19610
(610)375-6555
The BCMSA is exclusively an educational and charitable organization that focuses on community health. It encourages volunteerism and health related charitable activities.

Geisinger Medical Center Resident's Auxiliary
http://sites.google.com/site/geisingerra/
The GMC Auxiliary offers spouses of residents and fellows the opportunity to meet friends and get involved in the community in Danville. They have monthly meetings and active playgroups. Their 'meals for moms' program is a great way to support new moms.

Montgomery County Medical Spouse Alliance
http://www.montmedsoc.com/Main-Menu-
Categories/About-Us/County-Alliance
491 Allendale Road, Ste. 323
King of Prussia, PA 19406
The MCMs Alliance supports community health education, provides scholarships for health majors. They encourage the establishment of lifelong friendships through their support of the medical family and the unique challenges that it faces.

Northampton County Medical Society Alliance
http://www.ncmsa.org/
PO Box 21271
Lehigh Valley, PA 18002-1271
The NCMSA is a social organization that offers its members the opportunity to also participate in community health education projects.

Pennsylvania Medical Society Alliance
http://www.pamedsoc.org/MainMenuCategories/Re
sources/AffiliatedOrganizations/Alliance.aspx
The PMSA motto is "Physician spouses dedicated to the health of America". They are the parent organization to 28 county alliances throughout the state.

South Carolina

Medical University of South Carolina Residents Auxiliary
http://colleges.musc.edu/gmehandbook/administration_
governance/res_auxiliary.html
The MUSC Resident's Auxiliary is a support group for the spouses
of resident physicians at the Medical University of South
Carolina. They offer a variety of social activities including
playgroups, parties, regular meetings, outings and the
opportunity to get involved in charitable work.

South Carolina Medical Association Alliance
https://www.scmedical.org/content/alliance
The SCMAA supports the South Carolina Medical Association by
working to provide patients in the community with access to
high quality healthcare, while supporting physicians and the
greater goals of the American Medical Association.

Tennessee

Tennessee Medical Association Alliance
www.tmaalliance.org
2301 21st Avenue South
Nashville, TN 37212
(615) 460-1651
Toll Free: (800) 659-1862
The Tennessee Medical Association Alliance supports the Tennessee Medical Association through its education and community service programs. They support 16 local alliances throughout the state of Tennessee.

University of Tennessee Resident's Alliance
www.utra.org
This University of Tennessee in Knoxville spouse organization provides social support to spouses through playgroups, ladies nights out and a variety of volunteer and family activities. They are a sister organization to the Knoxville Academy of Medicine Alliance and dedicate themselves to the support of medical spouses as well as fostering a family friendly environment within the UT residency programs.

Texas

Bexar County Medical Spouse Alliance
www.bcmsalliance.org
6243 West IH-10, Suite 600
San Antonio, TX 78201
The Bexar County Medical Spouse Alliance located in San Antonio, TX is a community of medical families with a wide variety of activities for medical spouses and their families including a book club and a culinary capers club. They are active in health education programs within the community. Visit the BCMSA website for contact information.

Dallas County Medical Society Alliance
http://www.dcmsaf.org/DCMSA_web/Welcome.html
The DCMSA is honored with the title of oldest, continuously operating alliance in the United States. They offer a range of activities and community service opportunities to their members. Visit their website and browse through their newsletters for more information.

Denton County Medical Society Alliance
http://www.geocities.ws/dcmsa49/
Physician spouses joining to care is the motto for the DCMSA. The organization brings together the members of the Denton County Medical Society and is actively involved in volunteer activities within the community.

Resident Spouse Alliance of John Peter Smith Hospital
http://jpsrsa.blogspot.com
The RSPA aims to support the spouses of residents at John Peter Smith Hospital through social activities.

Tarrant County Medical Society Alliance and Foundation
http://www.tcmsalliance.org/
The TCMS Alliance is an organization which focuses on supporting the families of physicians while also encouraging community health education activities.

Texas Tech Medical Spouse Alliance
http://ttuhscmedicalalliance.blogspot.com
The Texas Tech Medical Spouse Alliance is a support group for the spouses of medical students and residents at Texas Tech University Health Science Center. They have a variety of activities scheduled throughout the year for families.

Travis County Medical Society Alliance
http://www.traviscountymedicalalliance.com/
The Travis County Medical Society Alliance is active in volunteer projects that focus on community health. Quality of life organizations within the alliance focus on supporting medical families. An outreach and support committee also helps medical families undergoing crisis.

Utah

Utah Medical Association Alliance
http://umaaweb.org/
The UMA supports the Utah Medical Association and is the parent organization to Cache, Carbon, Davis, Iron, Salt Lake, Utah, Washington and Weber county alliances.

Utah Partners in Medicine
www.utahpim.com
The PIM program at the University of Utah is an organization that supports interns, residents, fellows and their significant others. They have interest groups ranging from book clubs to guys and ladies nights out as well as ski clubs, wine clubs and more. Members can get involved in community service projects and find out information about the Salt Lake City Area. The annual dues are $15.

Virginia

Medical Society of Virginia Alliance
http://alliance.msv.org/
The MSVA is an affiliate of the Medical Society of Virginia. They provide friendship and support to medical families while supporting community programs which encourage healthy living to improve the quality of life for all people.

Richmond Academy of Medicine Alliance
http://www.ramaf.org
P.O. Box 70933
Richmond, VA 23255
RAMA is branch of the Medical Society of Virginia Alliance. Members of the alliance can take part in community health projects or get involved in legislative advocacy. There are monthly meetings and social activities for medical families. Annual dues are $100.

West Virginia

West Virginia State Medical Association Alliance
http://www.wvsma.com/AboutUs/WVSMAAlliance.aspx
WVSMA Alliance, Inc.

4307 MacCorkle Ave, S.E.
P.O. Box 4106
Charleston, WV 25364

The WVSMA is the parent organization for alliances in Cabell County, Eastern Panhandle, Harrison County, Kanawha County, Logan County, Mercer County, Monongalia County, Ohio County and Raleigh County. The organization dedicates itself to the health of all West Virginia ns while focusing on the strength of the medical family as well.

Wisconsin

Medical College of Wisconsin Resident Spouse Association
http://www.mcw.edu/display/router.asp?docid=2431
The primary focus of the RSA is to provide medical spouse with support and fun social activities during the medical training years. Enjoy monthly meetings, playgroups, kid's activities, and find information about area neighborhoods. Membership is $30/year.

University of Wisconsin House Staff Association
http://www.uwha.org/viewid.asp?pageid=19
Join the UWHA to meet other spouses who are sharing the experience of medical training. This is a significant other organization that welcomes all spouses. The organization encourages community outreach activities as well as participation in social activities.

Wisconsin Medical Society Alliance
https://www.wisconsinmedicalsociety.org/about-us/strategic-partners/alliance/
330 E. Lakeside Street PO Box 1109
Madison, WI 53701
(608) 442-3737
Members of the WMSA can volunteer for programs encourage healthy living. For more information about the alliance, visit the website or contact the alliance office.

International Organizations

The following list of resources provides information about medical spouse and family support programs outside of the United States of America

Australia

NSW Rural Medical Family Network
www.rmfn.org.au/site/index.cfm
203 Kelly Street
Scone NSW 2337
Australia
Phone: 02 6545 2461
The NSW Rural Medical Family Network addresses the needs of medical spouses in New South Wales, Australia. The organization provides newsletters, meetings, conferences, crisis assistance for medical families and financial assistance to spouses wishing to retrain professionally.

Queensland Rural Medical Family Network
www.qrmfn.com.au
The Queensland Rural Medical Family Network was established to support the needs of medical spouses in Queensland's rural communities. They offer a variety of family events and are establishing a spouse mentoring program.

Rural Health West
www.ruralhealthwest.com.au/go/support/families
P.O.Box 433
Nedlands
Western Australia 6909
Rural Western Australia provides support to physician spouses through volunteer area representatives. Social events, family programs and telephone counseling services are also provided.

Victorian Rural Medical Family Network
www.rmfn-vic.com
Level 3, 480 Collins Street
Melbourne
Victoria 3000
Phone: (61 3) 8610 6318
The Victorian Rural Medical Family Network provides opportunities for medical spouses in rural Victoria Australia to connect with each other through the development of spouse programs, newsletters and conferences.

Caribbean Islands

American University of the Caribbean Spouse Support
http://aucspousesorganization.wordpress.com/
Visit the AUC Support organization to connect with other spouses on the island. The organization has a cooking club, playgroups, book club and beach a week activity. Their website is a rich resource of information about life on the island as well as activities available for families. In addition, they have their own message forum.

S.O.S
http://www.sabamed.org/sos/Sos.html
Spouses of Medical Students at Saba University School of Medicine can find encouragement, support and information from SOS. This is a network that supports spouses of medical students and faculty members through meetings and activities geared towards the medical spouse. A detailed survival guide is available at the website that provides spouses with information about living on Saba.

Significant Other Organization
http://sites.google.com/site/soorgsgu/Home
The SOO at St. George's University is an activity community that supports the spouses of students studying abroad in Grenada, West Indies. Their website provides information about volunteer opportunities and a play group as well as forums to ask specific questions.

Appendix 3
General Websites for Medical Families

A variety of websites are available that address important issues facing medical students, residents, fellows and their families. The following is a list of website resources for the medical family.

The Accreditation Council for Graduate Medical Education
www.acgme.org
The Accreditation Council for Graduate Medical Education (AGCME) is responsible for evaluating and accrediting residency and fellowship programs in the United States. Their website provides information about the review and accreditation process as well as information on how residents can file a formal complaint about residency program non-compliance with accreditation guidelines.

FREIDA Online
http://www.ama-assn.org/ama/pub/category/2997.html
FREIDA Online is a searchable database provided by the American Medical Association. The database provides information on over 7800 accredited residency and fellowship programs.

MomMD
www.mommd.com
MomMD is a professional and social networking website for women and mothers in medicine. Their active forums provide areas for pre-medical students, medical students, residents and attending physicians.

NRMP
www.nrmp.org
The National Resident Matching Program is a website that every medical family should become well-acquainted with. Find information about the general *Match* including dates, fees and charts of the general outcomes for prior 'match' participants.

OldPreMeds
www.oldpremeds.net
The National Society for Nontraditional Premedical and Medical Students is the premier website for older students and their families. Find information about getting into medical school as a nontraditional applicant as well as a supportive forum community. Annual meetings have become a hallmark of this longstanding web-based community.

ScutWork
www.scutwork.com
ScutWork is a website that provides ratings for many residency and fellowship programs. Ratings are based on program teaching, atmosphere and research. Information about resident schedules is also documented.

The Student Doctor Network
www.studentdoctor.net
The Student Doctor Network (SDN) is the largest community of students in healthcare professions. Their message forums are an excellent resource for individuals in all stages of the medical training process.

Residency and Fellowship
www.residencyandfellowship.com
The Residency and Fellowship website presents information about applying for residency, and hosts a forum with information about the USMLE and medical licensing issues.

USMLE
www.usmle.org
The United States Medical Licensing Exam website provides detailed information about the USMLE exams

References

Part 1

Chapter1

Burns and Moss. *Somebody's Getting Married/She'll Make Me Happy.* 1984

Part 2

Autumn 2010 Survey of Resident/Fellow Stipends and Benefits. [WWW document]. URL https://www.aamc.org/download/158738/data/2010_stipend_report.pdf

Chapter 12
Chatzky, Jean. *Building a Budget.* [WWW document]. URL http://www.practicalmoneyskills.com/budgeting

SunTrust Bank. Loan Limits and Repayment Options.[WWW document].URLwww.suntrust.com/portal/server.pt/community/rate_terms_conditions/559

Chapter 13
American Medical Student Association. Medical Student Debt. [WWW document]. URL http://www.amsa.org/meded/studentdebt.cfm

Quotations

Cook, John. *The Book of Positive Quotations*. Minneapolis, MN:
Fairview Press, 1997.
DeFord, Deborah. Quotable Quotes. Pleasantville, New York:
Reader's Digest Association, Inc., 1997.

Index

C and B Press

Live it, Write it, Share it!

CPSIA information can be obtained at www.ICGtesting.com
Printed in the USA
BVOW03s2221191113

336787BV00004B/36/P